CONTENTS

AUTHOR'S PREFACE

In The Grip of Necrocapitalism looks at the human condition through a wide frame of reference which covers not only our accomplishments, but also the tragic failures which have led to the global collapse of industrial civilisation currently taking place. While traditional history and anthropology tend to focus on how we got from point A to point Z, this book will be focusing on how we got from A to Zero, via Z. Because it is precisely our accomplishments which have been our downfall, therefore raising the need for a fresh post-mortem account of events that can attempt to integrate accomplishments and downfalls as part of one, cohesive story which resonates whichever way one may choose to read it: front to back, or back to front. This is the story of how we became victims of, and slaves to, our own ambitions.

Undoubtedly there is a lot of volume to unpack, and the mere exposure of our human failures is only the tip of the iceberg in this rapidly unfolding situation. A book about humans written by a human couldn't possibly remove all human-centric bias, nor can an author living in our current dystopia be fully aware of just how dystopian our civilisation has already become. But in order to minimize any subconscious bias, the author doesn't hesitate to question and scrutinize everything we know, or we thought we knew, about our history and our role on this planet: from our humble beginnings as a single cell floating in a pool of sludge, to today's tech fascism-dominated digital dystopia.

Beware that after you have read this book, your view of the world may drastically change. Once you've had a good look behind the parapet of the pretty, fake, colorful, consumer entertainment metaverse our current custodians

1

have meticulously curated for us, there is no going back. You have now seen the truth. If you prefer to wait behind the door and enjoy the metaverse, that's fine. But for those of us seeking closure, answers, maybe even fragments of redemption from our spectacular evolutionary dead end, the ideas in this book may as well provide the vital reckoning with our past which needs to happen first and foremost, before any discussion or action, even if it may already be too late.

Delving deeper while at the same time zooming further out from some of the concepts explored in my previous book, The Unhappiness Machine, In The Grip of Necrocapitalism explores a rapidly evolving situation of capitalism having merged with intelligent technology, and the far-reaching implications of this chimeric monstrosity. This is an entity of our own creation, one which we falsely thought would make us safer and more powerful. Ironically, just as we approach the apex of our technological culmination, things are beginning to take a sharp, karmic turn for the worst: this new and emerging entity, one which has never existed before on this planet, is now doing to us what we did to the planet and its beings a long time ago. It is an increasingly sentient, mutationally adaptable, self-learning form of capitalism which is slowly, but steadily, becoming our owner by cleverly using consumerism, automation, surveillance and an ever more inventive, not to mention addictive, range of technological narcotics which turn us into nothing but hedonistic consumatrons.

As you open the door that lies beyond these pages, you may need to take a deep breath, even though the air is unsafe. Because this is the only air you'll have. You can take in the wide vista of our current dystopia, free from the colour filters of the mind prison which controls us. You may want to ignore the door, and simply wait until it explodes, unable to hold back the melting furnace behind it. Or, as a naturally curious human, you might as well crack it open just a bit, and begin to seek for yourself the answers you desperately need about why, after so much evolution, progress and innovation, we are where we are today in our dark predicament.

In The Grip of Necrocapitalism makes the macabre observation that we are not heading for a collapse. We are experiencing the symptoms of a collapse which started long ago, and whose effects have been filtering through our complex system for a while. This process consists of the collapse of the fabric which kept the ecology of this planet together, as well as an almost complete collapse of human spiritual consciousness, something which is doubtful whether we ever possessed in the first place.

If you do decide to open this door, please do it with compassion towards yourself. By merely recognizing the existence of the door, you have already come a long way in terms of enlightenment, consciousness, and infinite, expansive, unconditional, true love.

George Tsakraklides

Kavala, Greece, October 2023

NECROGLOSSARY

Algorithmocracy
A techno-fascist political system whereby highly sophisticated algorithms manipulate public opinion in order to control power. Self-trained on microtargetted communications using consumatrons' digital footprint, the algorithms can personify themselves as human and easily achieve specific propaganda objectives requiring very minimal initial human input. The algorithmocracy can eventually become autonomous.

BOE
(Bank of Earth). The only solvent bank system that has existed on Earth, run as a cooperative by 8 million species who all hold an equal stake. The BOE is the one and only lender of the parasitic human economy (the psychonomy), which has operated at a net loss since its existence.

Suicide Economics
A boom-and-bust model of growth where a parasitic economy overexerts itself to achieve quick profit, flatlines, then uses external bailouts from the BOE in order to build itself back up. The risk of suicide economics is the long-term solvency of the BOE, which knows no boom and bust cycles. Unlike the human economy, once it is bust, it is bust.

Biochauvinism
Any prejudice arising from the attempt to compare two very different life forms based on subjective, usually unfairly selected criteria. The objective of the comparison is usually to establish human supremacist narratives of conflict and domination, which can be weaponized by colonialism and necrocapitalism.

Cakeconomics
An aggressive profit-making model whereby damaging and unethical practices are used to lower production costs and meet increasing consumer demand, while at the same time huge quantities of unsold product end up in landfills. Cakeconomics follows the maximum death / maximum profit necrocapitalist principle in order to increase both product turnover and profit.

Consumatron
A modern human out of touch with their inner world, who has lost the ability to experience joy outside of the realm of compulsive consumption and manufactured entertainment.

EoT
(Earthnet of Things) The planet's own surveillance and internal communications network, comprised of all interconnected biotic, abiotic, geological and chemical processes. Everything on Earth is part of the EoT, including humans.

Human Farming
The progressive and systematic rearing of humans under closely monitored conditions for the sole purpose of converting them into consumatrons. The farm is a business which needs to ensure that consumatrons continue purchasing the mass-manufactured goods of the psychonomy, as well as give birth to multiple offspring which will continue to support both the production and consumption of these products.

The Great Procrastination
The tendency of each psychonomic civilisation to pass down to its successor all of the long-term issues it has inherited from its predecessors, which it has chosen to ignore e.g. the climate crisis and all aspects of overshoot.

Mind Prison
A programmable, safe space within the brain which can censor incoming stimuli and completely block access to reality.

Money
A loan from the BOE, to humans.

Necrocapitalism
The acceleration of the death of life forms and resources via single-use technologies, expiration dates, product obsolescence and maximum profit / maximum death economics. By devaluing beings and resources, necrocapitalism is able to apply the maximum possible sales margin.

Nitrous Media
Media channels which apply a comedy veneer on news, facts, social commentary or opinion in order to downgrade, normalize, distort, and effectively censor it.

Numerization
The conversion of qualitative and subjective concepts such as happiness or employee performance into falsely measurable quantities and metrics. Numerization is a sweeping trend across all facets of civilisation and is a sign of the increasingly algorithmic nature of the psychonomy.

Psychonomy
An economic system which is heavily reliant upon the commercialization and exploitation of the mental disorders of both its workers and its end consumers.

Religion
One of the marketing departments of the psychonomy.

Replacement Economics
The profitable approach of solving issues by replacing the

technology, rather than addressing the issue itself. Although the benefits to society and the environment range from negligible to incremental, profits can be huge for investors. It is not uncommon for side effects of the new technology to emerge, resulting in a compounding of the original issue which the technology was attempting (pretending) to solve in the first place.

Supermarketization

The conversion of natural resources and life forms, including humans, into monetizable assets with no rights or sovereignty of their own. Supermarketization is a key facet of necrocapitalism.

The Thing

A non-biological, rapidly mutating, self-learning new economic management entity which has seized operation of the psychonomy and follows exclusively necrocapitalist principles. The Thing is almost omnipresent, in similarity to the EoT. Humans are the original engineers of The Thing, but increasingly becoming demoted to "appointed managers".

The Unhappiness Machine

The merging of manufacturing, logistics, marketing, advertising and algorithm-based psychology into an entity which invents unhappiness on an industrial scale, optimizes it, then mines it for profit via consumer products and services.

DELUSIONS OF INDEPENDENCE

Problem Child

It has been eons since humans committed the ultimate ecosystem hubris: to dare go it alone, leaving behind the 8 million-strong species they had co-evolved with. Like rebellious teenagers, clueless of what they wanted to do with their lives, they dashed out the back window one night, abandoning the family who had nurtured them for 3.8 billion years. Entering the unknown, they hid amongst the dark shadows at the edge of the ecosystem, where they began to morph into a bizarre, sometimes beautiful, but undoubtedly sinister new world: one that was selfishly intended for humans, and humans only.

Prompted more by impulse than thoughtful deliberation, the teenagers had forever left behind their little village, trading it in for the big, ugly city they were about to erect. Free from the rules and supervision of the ecosystem, they could now mold their new environment any which way they wanted: keeping it as untidy as they liked, surviving on drugs, junk food and rock n' roll. They had finally gotten what they wished for, which was to break the rules of the ecosystem, leave all of nature behind, and try to forget the place they had come from as quickly as possible, as if it had all been one, big, ugly nightmare.

The city's architectural style would become a bold statement of independence from nature, as well as a full-on affront, a declaration of war towards Earth itself. It was a vision of a city that was so ugly, so inhospitable to life that no species would ever dare to dwell in it except for humans. As a matter of fact, within the confines of the city, the teenagers had indeed managed to banish almost all life forms, bar the occasional ornamental tree or lingering "pest". Without nature's artistic input to illuminate the dark, urban corners, or soften the sharp, austere spikes of human arrogance, new structures called "buildings" would emerge and evolve into nameless, stiff and desolate monolithic monuments of untold brutality. These were the new homes of people, secluded on all sides by thick, impenetrable walls which were pretty much sound proof, weather proof, and life proof. The occasional window or balcony would allow some light in, though the typical view was either of another building or a busy polluted road.

Humans tried to give these cities names, so that people would feel less intimidated and visit them. But as the cities grew in size further and further, the teenagers' urban vision would come true: the city would become a place exclusively for humans, given that no other species on Earth would tolerate so much toxicity, noise and violence on a daily basis - 100% of it self-inflicted. Luckily, humans were extremely resourceful and could tolerate this environment. They were so busy with their lives anyway, that they could not see the ugliness they had created.

It must have taken immense greed and ambition on the part of the architects of the city to be so blind to pollution and destruction, and to come to believe that somehow this sterile, desolate and toxic landscape was a vision of progress, an investment into the future, and a place where they would eventually bring up their children. By building megacities, humans had succeeded in shutting nature out while at the same time creating a prison for themselves.

While impressive as an engineering feat, the story of the city had been one of annihilation and extinction all along. Today, humanity is responsible for the existence of some of the most abysmally ugly and depressing, hostile, toxic and dangerous environments on Earth, most of them created on lands that were once part of the richest, most habitable and biologically diverse zones of this planet. Lush river deltas, fertile valleys, sun-kissed coastlines once buzzing with an almost infinite array of life forms, were aggressively taken over and replaced by monocultures of humans who offered nothing to the local landscape, other than mechanically reproducing more and more copies of themselves.

But however ugly, inhospitable, and sterile the city was, it would easily manage to charm humans right from the beginning with its imposing grandeur and illuminated evening vistas. The city dwellers would admire the city and feel proud as humans for having created this monstrous, bizarre new world. The city would become a symbol of their independence, a living reminder that they had "made it": they had escaped nature, safe inside their industrial concrete fortresses.

Sitting on this narrative of accomplishment and power, and comparing themselves to the Creator, the teenage humans were able to continue to feed their delusion of independence: that they didn't need the village anymore, even though it continued to be the source of all their food, oxygen and water. They had created their own little single-species ecosystem, unaware that it was merely a parasite of the ecosystem they had come from.

Psychonomic Civilisations

For the teenagers, everything outside of the city was nothing but a cheap resource to be exploited, and their arrogance grew day by day as they descended into a spiral of addiction and mental illness, often exacerbated by the city itself. Instead of abandoning their concrete fortress and returning to the village, they would choose to stay there, in this concrete hell, and somehow build their life upon, and around, their mounting addictions, obsessions, and psychoses. In order to work around their mental turmoil, they would in fact end up creating a civilization where all of these psychoses were not only considered normal, but would eventually become useful skills. They would become the bedrock of social and political organisation. This would be a civilization where the most psychotic and unstable personalities were welcomed and, would in fact thrive and attain leadership positions. They would be the most successful individuals, leading the way for humanity and enabling people to live not necessarily a happy, but at least a functional existence within these brutal, soul-destroying cities. These highly psychotic, yet highly successful individuals, would keep the city going and ensure the growth and establishment of humanity's economic system, the psychonomy: a place where almost any and every psychosis is a talent waiting to blossom.

But the problem with highly urbanized societies is that personal happiness was defined largely in relation to the closest neighbor's possessions and achievements. There is absolutely nothing personal or "real" about this type of happiness. There was always another neighbor who had more wealth, and who became yet another reason to feel unhappy. The city's residents would consequently sink into further unhappiness, which made them pursue more addictions and psychotic behaviours. This of course made the psychonomy stronger, more diverse, more resilient. It began to grow together with humanity's escalating psychoses, forming an intricate and increasingly specialised economic web of mutual exploitation. Civilisation became incredibly complex.

Today, humans have become resigned and adapted to the anxiety, depression, greed, schizophrenia and loneliness that they have largely brought upon themselves. They have successfully erected a civilization, economy and society which are almost exclusively powered by a wide assortment of mental illnesses, masterfully disguised and rebranded as skills, talents and inclinations. This is why, although many people are successful, they still feel that something is missing: their long-gone sanity. Our civilization has been built on the successful exploitation not only of our talents, but our psychoses too. All of us to an extent have made a career out of the multiple psychoses that undoubtedly come with having such a huge brain.

If at any point a citizen of the city wakes up and realizes that they are in fact mentally unstable, there are many painkillers which can help them go back to their "happy" sleep: drugs, alcohol, Netflix, and an endless, almost infinite assortment of consumer products which will distract them, and reward them for being such a good sport for taking all of this mentally-burdening urban abuse on the chin.

Generations of Estrangement

Back in the village, the cherry trees that bloom every spring, the goldfish in the pond, have no idea that they've been turned into villains. They live in fear that their grown-up teenager may one day come back to the village and burn it all down, turn the trees into furniture, the fish into sushi for corporate egomaniacs' business lunch breaks. The junkie teenager intends to sell the village all off, in order to buy more drugs.

As the psychonomy expanded, the planet suffered the tragic consequences of humans having effectively domesticated themselves within their own asylum, then outsourced this domestication to The Thing: an economic management entity hungry for data, which is now breeding estranged generations of increasingly brainwashed, unhealthy human cattle: all of them unaware of what they have done to themselves, to the planet, and of what is yet to come.

Most of humanity today still thinks like a teenager. It continues to hold the belief that turning our back on nature was not only the right decision, but a natural and unavoidable progression for our species. The teenager may have grown up, but they are more stubborn and selfish than ever, and ever more hateful towards the family they abandoned long ago. They've had their own kids by now, who have grown up entirely in the city, and who harbour an even more naïve and estranged relationship with nature, unaware of its importance in keeping the city alive.

In fact, to them nature is an alien world somewhere far out in the distance. They have no ecological conscience, because all they have ever known is the tiny concrete bubble of the city. They don't know that this bubble is nested within a much bigger, more important one, Earth's global ecology. Ecology is bigger than capitalism, bigger than human civilization itself. Yet for most humans today, ecology takes place somewhere in the sidelines of our existence, or in a classroom, or a nature documentary. We fail to grasp the gravity of our ignorance of basically almost everything that exists, having eyes and ears only for what happens inside our tiny artificial bubble which we arrogantly call "civilisation".

The Deluded Predator

Desperate to prop-up its delusions about its estrangement, as it matured over the course of millennia our teenage civilization would go on to masterfully craft countless false narratives about human supremacy over nature, which it vilified as a wild, hostile beast to be tamed, subordinated and eliminated by trophy hunters. The grown-up teenager today still uses these narratives to convince themselves that they had made the right decision to leave the village. These narratives are the lullabies they sing to their unsuspecting children, every time it becomes momentarily clear that humans in fact may have failed not only their original family, but also themselves and their children, and that these cities are in fact killing them. The self-serving narratives of the teenager only manage to further inflate their ego. A predator who has no natural enemies eventually becomes so arrogant and narcissistic that they build a prison around them, thinking it's a palace.

The city has now grown so much that its inhabitants are completely ignorant of what lies beyond it. The edges of the city are expanding as they blindly consume the countryside, like an unstoppable fungus on its way to completing its lifecycle. Arrogantly obsessed with growth, human civilization has no idea that it is already finished. It is spending imaginary money it doesn't have on resources which are permanently disappearing, to raise a generation of humans who will soon be fighting for food.

Amongst all of our achievements, the planet's destruction risks becoming our ultimate legacy, casting its shadow over anything and everything we have ever accomplished. Any trip to the moon, brilliant invention or work of art ever created by humans will pale in comparison to the colossal damage we inflicted on an infinitely complex network of diverse, interconnected ecosystems which used to span the entirety of this planet - much of them already gone. All of this, so that we can be independent.

Our New, Infinite Loneliness

But while humans continued to achieve impressive accomplishments within their busy cities, they had failed to evolve all parts of themselves. If anything, they had been devolving further into a psychotic mess. What they had lost most of all, was the ability to feel joy without having to manufacture it, rationalise it, or analyse it. By rejecting nature, the teenagers wanted to assert their independence. What they discovered instead was a new kind of infinite loneliness, living in a biodiverse-poor world which they had largely made extinct.

Humans today are not only lonely, but increasingly alone on the planet as more and more of our family is driven to extinction. Even parasites need friends: they are part of the ecosystem which they need for their survival. Their existence depends wholly upon the hosts they have infected, who become part of the jury in their final reckoning. Humanity is becoming a lonely, dislocated parasite, while at the same time learning the macabre task of parasitizing itself. It will eventually run out of fuel to throw into its demented inferno, but by the time this happens the damage will have been almost complete. The fire of our automated, necrocapitalist psychonomic system will only stop once it has burned just about everything.

Whether we are a parasite or not, as more of our family members across the seven biological kingdoms disappear, we are left without our life support. Earth only works as a federation of 8 million species, not a dictatorship of one. As this civilization approaches its natural disintegration, the teenager will soon lose their job, go bankrupt, and will need a home to return to, but this home won't be there. They will be going back to a burned down village with no resources. Only then might they realize that there was never a reason to leave in the first place. They had all they could ever wish for, back at the village. But instead of building their life as part of the ecosystem, they had given up their connections, their relationship to nature, to pursue a selfish fantasy which only a blind heart can create. The fantasy became reality, in the cruelest of ways: the teenagers wanted to go it alone, and this is what they got in the end: ending up surrounded by desolate urban wastelands where humans lived close to one another, but barely interacted.

Reducing our view of nature to a mere peripheral part of our existence has not only been naïve and arrogant, but a death wish which is beginning to materialize. The more estranged from their roots new generations of humans become, the more diabetes, Alzheimer's, sterility and a myriad of new and emerging mental and physical illnesses of our necrocapitalist world will afflict them, guaranteeing that the door to the future among those who survive remains firmly shut.

Well over a third of Earth's current habitable land area has been modified by human civilisation, to create either cities or arable land. Much of it is becoming either too hot to support life, or turning into ocean or desert. The entire planet is being transformed by human overpopulation, and the resulting climate catastrophe. This is what happens to a civilisation when it rests its foundations upon the most imperialistic, narcissistic and egotistical tendencies.

It is these psychoses which have kept feeding our delusion of independence, and which are still, to this day, the most vital "skill sets" in our greed-obsessed psychonomy. The various chapters in this book explore different facets of these psychoses, many of which have been with us since the beginning of our journey.

THE FALSE NARRATIVE OF CONFLICT

Evolving Into One

3.5 billion years ago, life began to emerge on Earth. A single, lonely cell, the ancestor which we share with every other life form on the planet, began to diverge into unique individual species. At first, only a handful of fragile life forms existed, barely distinguishable from each other. Fast forward a few million years, and an incredible diversity of life emerged, enough to provide material for countless hours of David Attenborough documentaries.

Yet many of the natural world's wonders remain undiscovered today, at an age when we arrogantly think that we have seen it all, and catalogued it all in our documentaries, encyclopedias, museums and genetic banks. We naively think that we have a thorough understanding of Earth's infinite diversity and complexity, simply by recording, cataloguing and capturing everything in pixels, bytes and megabytes. But we still have very little understanding of what an ecosystem is, and how it has come into existence. Examining the individual parts of this system does very little in helping us understand how the sum of it all functions.

This is because as species diversified further, they began to form incredibly complex relationships with each other, and here is where the beautiful paradox emerged: the more they evolved and diverged, becoming bacteria, birds, fish, fungi, terrestrial mammals or insects, the more they became one superorganism, consisting of intricate yet extremely intimate relationships between the species, vital to each other's survival. Ironically, the more all these species evolved, the more they remained as one. Throughout this long evolutionary journey they had remained functioning as that one, initial organism, even as they split into more and more individual, differentiated species.

Our traditional textbook representation of a phylogenetic tree of free-standing branches misses out on this important concept of oneness, unity and interdependence. It fails to capture the interrelationship of species belonging to different branches of the tree, both within the physical environments they co-inhabit, as well as the gene sequences they share. Evidence has been accumulating about the feasibility of lateral transfer of genes across genera, and even between animal kingdoms - that is, the exchange of genetic information between species located in distant, completely unrelated branches of the tree - usually through various "accidents" and vectors. The discovery of more and more examples of these direct gene transfers suggests that these are not "freak" events, but part of an evolutionary process which is more dynamic, mysterious, unpredictable and innovative than we had originally thought.

Yet this is something which, until relatively recently, was thought impossible as it didn't follow the snail pace of traditional Darwinian evolution through single-point DNA mutations. What this evidence comes down to is that, the branches of the phylogenetic tree do not always end up nowhere, as they do in a real tree. They sometimes reconnect to the roots of the genetic tree, and they can also link back into each other, in strange and unexpected ways which we are only just beginning to uncover. This tree is much more connected than we had assumed.

It is as if the primordial soup - that thick, murky sludge of chemicals out of which the first living organism on the planet came into existence - is in some ways still in operation: randomly churning, combining proto-molecules into novel, magical, gene sequences. The planet's genetic code is perhaps a lot more maleable than we had thought. There is a certain freedom of information which allows nature to experiment, and sometimes "beta-test" the same exact gene in a different organism so that it can see if it may be useful elsewhere, or even re-purpose it for a new task, with the odd mutation here and there. It is not uncommon to find almost identical gene sequences in different organisms, serving completely different functions - yet obviously having descended from the same original sequence. Some of them were even formerly "evil" genes belonging to viruses: viruses tend to often function as the "USB sticks" of the planet's genetic pool: accidentally integrating their DNA into their host, and super-charging the evolutionary process by means of literally re-writing or disrupting the host's DNA in one, big, copy and paste job.

Without going too much into the science, the implication of all this is that, aside from sharing distant ancestors, it is possible that we share even more with other species on Earth, species which we traditionally regard as barely related to us. There is even more unity between organisms in Earth's family tree than we had initially assumed. All species are "different and same" at the same time, and undoubtedly connected and dependent upon each other for their survival. As this genetic pool which everyone has been drawing from becomes increasingly extinct, everyone loses - not just those going extinct.

The Invisible Superorganism

In our obsession to focus on the differences between species as we catalogued them through the ages, we had literally missed the forest for the trees, or more accurately, the tree for the branches: we had failed to pay attention to how these species are connected and related, and we began to study them as independent organisms living in isolation, as opposed to components within a much bigger, much more complex superorganism. It was like taking apart a car and studying a specific part, e.g. the wheel, without having any concept of where this wheel goes on the car, what its function is, and how it works together with the other car parts. The wheel by itself means absolutely nothing, has very little worth or significance, if it is not understood within the context of the ecosystem of other car parts it belongs to. Yet our traditional science has focused on the wheel, all by itself: how round it is, what its made of, and so on, giving ourselves the false impression that we know this wheel, when in fact we know absolutely nothing about either its past or its present.

The superorganism is therefore not just a sum of the branches on the genetic tree, but also of all the interconnections and cooperations between the species, which include the important context of each life form: the specific role it is expected to play within the superorganism. This complex web of connections is the superorganism itself, a descendant of that one, monocellular life form which started it all. In a way, our common monocellular ancestor never really split into independent species. It simply became more complex. Yet this superorganism, which is by far the most important, the most complex of them all, is invisible to humans. We have yet to acknowledge and appreciate its existence, even though we, humans, are a part of it.

The Myth of The Predator

Although appearing to be chaotic on the surface, our ecosystem is at the same time incredibly simple and balanced in its operating principles. When studying either the ecosystem or the climate system, humans tend to focus on chaos and conflict, either between species or between weather elements. This is because they are again making the mistake of thinking of species as independent and isolated. They see them as competitors, and overlook the overall harmony which keeps the superorganism alive and functioning. They try to explain their observations of the ecosystem based on the principle of interspecies competition and conflict, rather than appreciating that these competing species also need each other at the same time. There is an overarching harmony and flat structure which presides over the entire ecosystem, yet humans have always been on a mission to understand nature through narratives of conflict: "who is on top" and "who is at the bottom" of the food chain.

We seem to only want to understand the ecosystem as a series of power struggles and bitter rivalries, as opposed to balanced relationships between natural competitors who share the various resources of the planet. It is no wonder then that we have destroyed much of Earth's ecosystem already, having viewed our role as that of a warrior in a conflict where there are only two options: to kill, or be killed. We consider ourselves predators, when in fact every species within Earth's ecosystem is both a predator and prey. The ultimate predator is Earth: it decides whether a species still has what it takes to remain on the planet. If it crosses a line, or has nothing to offer anymore to the other species, it is naturally phased out.

Unity Within The Chaos

This means that although species are indeed often engaged in brutal conflict as they antagonize each other, consume each other, or compete for the same habitat, they are all at the same time still part of the superorganism, which has remained in perfect health for countless millennia. Resources within this superorganism are finite and fairly distributed so that, despite all of the competition, everyone has enough to eat in the end. The truth is, there are no winners or losers, predator or prey, sentient or non-sentient life forms in the ecosystem. There is only balance and unity. We, the life forms of this planet, are all connected. All we are is matter which travels from one being to the next.

Rather than celebrating the chemical and genetic heritage which connects us to other beings, humans have been poisoning the very circle which ultimately links back to them: by viewing our ecosystem through the "human supremacy lens" of conflict and competition, we have predisposed our own very toxic and aggressive relationship with the planet. Our track record is one of destruction and extinction, because this is the natural role that we see for ourselves. Yet many humans still like to see themselves as benevolent custodians of this planet, a patronizing, deluded and narcissistic view of who we are.

A Civilisation Built from Violence and Inequality

In the name of these human-centric narratives of conflict, we have committed unfathomable crimes towards the millions of other species who had an equal stake in this planet, ever since its creation. The complete annihilation of entire ecosystems sheltering millions of species, was not a side effect of civilisation. It was a deliberate crime perpetrated by the greatest minds, leaders and technologies humanity has produced.

Extinction is not something you can repair or ever apologize for. The minute we make another organism extinct, we are forever cursed until the end of time. Extinction is a one-way permanent exile from a genetic pool which took 3.8 billion years to build. We have chased far too many precious species down this shameful path to oblivion, for far too long. They have done nothing to us to deserve this. Yet rather than seeing other life forms as family members we depend upon, we have treated them as either food or obstacles for elimination. This conflict with the natural world is, and has always been, a manufactured narrative. It is a figment of our imagination – yet one that has been vital in sustaining the expansion of our ecocidal civilisation through slash and burn colonialism, capitalism and the manipulative lies of religion. Our focus on conflict, rather than balance, was key to civilizational expansion, which needed narratives of conflict, violence and supremacy over other species in order to justify its destruction-driven growth.

Establishing and maintaining inequality was key: there is always more profit to be made from the weak, rather than those less desperate. Our psychonomy is largely based on cannibalism towards the less fortunate humans, as well as life forms who are unable to defend themselves or their territories as humans do. What we call civilization would collapse without its dark side: the exploitation, monetization, and weaponization of the misfortune of those with less mental and physical capital - whether they are humans or non-humans.

Throughout their history, empires relied on these narratives of conflict, hastily and clumsily woven upon racial or species differences in order to give themselves the licence to destroy, to grow and to sustain their expansion. Our political, social and religious institutions were founded upon these narratives as well, which they have used for the subjugation of other species and human races ever since. Our popular culture today still largely relies on narratives of conflict with nature and superiority of humans over all other species, as this is the popular narrative which serves the human supremacy dogma, and maintains humanity's delusional ambitions about its place, and its future on this planet.

The Corruption of Science

Our psychonomy has tried to normalize this narrative of conflict and superiority as much as possible, and undoubtedly influenced how science works: reducing most scientists to butterfly collectors who study individual species in complete isolation - leaving the study of the most important aspect, the relationships between these species, to outsiders such as humanists, cosmologists, philosophers and off-beat ecologists.

Our academic obsession with cataloguing and recording other life forms is a very capitalist and objectified view of Earth and its species, aiming ultimately at human ownership and domination, whatever the specific science angle might be. Because of the commercial and human-centered angle of much of scientific research, the emphasis of our academic system has been not on understanding how we relate to all other beings on

Earth, that is, where we actually fit within the superorganism, but how we can study these other species so that we can best exploit them. Many of our academic institutions have stopped learning, and are profiting instead: making money for themselves, and for the necrocapitalist investors who back them. But when knowledge becomes a business, it is not knowledge anymore. It is the propaganda of those who sponsor it, and who select the "learnings" which best fit their agenda.

For humans, Earth is nothing but a huge supermarket: we are much more interested in owning nature, than understanding it. The planet's beings, now converted into products and placed on supermarket shelves, have no say on how much they are worth, and when they will expire. They have long ago lost any sovereignty whatsoever, and any rights to their own existence. This is a narrative which has served well all scientific endeavours, giving them the licence to destroy and disrupt, in the name of "knowledge" and discovery. As part of this narrative, and in order to do their science most effectively and impartially, scientists must bizarrely and perversely appear completely detached from their subject matter, even as they get closer and closer to it.

In fact, scientists are not allowed to get too close to their subject matter, in case they may become too emotional. There has to be zero emotion and zero connection. A climate scientist is not allowed to mourn the disappearance of an ancient glacier, except in their own private time away from publicity. The same goes for the scientist doing lethal experiments on animals. They are not allowed to let their emotions "interfere" with their scientific study, because these emotions will very likely interfere with the end application of the research findings, and upset the investors who funded the unethical research in the first place.

This disconnection of the researcher is dressed up as "scientific objectivity". We detach ourselves from the subject matter not because we want to be objective, but because we do not want to give "it" any rights of its own within the framework of the scientific study. The subject matter needs to become a passive, helpless "object", so that we can do to it whatever we please.

This pretentious objectivity is of course, a disguised human supremacy narrative: the superior, intelligent human, is the only one who can objectively study the inferior, much less intelligent organism: not as a life form with flesh, blood, emotions and sovereignty over its own body and soul, but as an object for personal use and abuse. This human supremacy narrative objectifies all organisms and does not even permit them to be "living", let alone exist as biological entities.

But they, just like us, are living beings, and they are extremely fragile. They have equal rights to us for access to the right temperature, food, and water at regular intervals. They have the same needs and entitlements to comfort and affection, however low in the "pecking order" of intelligence we decide to conveniently, and arbitrarily, place them.

Those who view nature and its beings as objects lack any palpable sense of who they are, what they are or even where they are. They spend their entire lives in an impenetrable darkness, living through millions of failed attempts to feel, see, and hear. In the end, they become objects themselves, half-filled vessels depleted of the elements which made them most "alive".

The More Differences, The More Power Structures

By adhering to these false narratives of conflict and supremacy, we have been focusing on the differences between species rather their similarities, as we desperately tried to create artificial hierarchies. The butterfly collector pays more attention to how butterfly species differ, as opposed to the attributes they share. The more sizes and colors of butterflies there are, the more exciting the chase becomes. The butterfly collector however, learns very little about butterflies through this process, even as his collection of victims grows. During this "knowledge chase", the butterfly collector ends up dumber and dumber, disconnected from the collective intelligence that he shares with his specimens, and which he will never quite grasp. He doesn't understand that both he and the butterfly are pieces of the superorgranism. Every time he is stabbing a butterfly on his clipboard, he is stabbing himself.

Our psychonomy wants us to be blind, mindless butterfly collectors who simply want to own and consume, focusing on what makes us different, than what brings us together. Only if we start focusing away from differences and observing the commonalities between species and human races, can the violent narratives of conflict upon which today's civilization was founded begin to dissolve.

Our psychonomy has needed these artificial narratives from its inception. It is because highlighting the differences between people and beings helps our system create power structures. Once these power structures are in place, they can be exploited. Morphological differences between species and between human races launched slavery, colonialism, extinction and countless wars, enabling empires to grow through an endless cycle of exploitation and destruction. These differences became the ideological bedrock behind religious and political structures which, were nothing but the marketing departments of the psychonomy. Racism is a prime example of how supremacy and conflict narratives were created and exploited, for purely economic reasons.

Conflict-Based Definitions of Intelligence

We therefore tend to seek differences, hierarchies and narratives of conflict all the time, so that we can find ways to dominate either over other species, or within our own. A particularly recurring theme across these narratives has always been the measurement of intelligence, or "sentience", because as it so happens, for most humans the level of intelligence of a species correlates with "how many rights" to life, to its own existence, it should have. This correlation between intelligence and the right to exist is completely arbitrary of course, and makes no sense whatsoever.

It wasn't randomly chosen though. Humans chose to "assign" the most rights to smarter species, because they consider themselves at the top of the intelligence ladder. The problem is that humans again, completely arbitrarily, have cherry-picked the criteria for evaluating and measuring intelligence which favour their own ranking. The truth however is that intelligence is neither measurable, nor is it comparable. Intelligence across species should not even be compared. A strawberry does different things from a seagull, and from a human. All three species are intelligent within their own niche, and the specific function they are meant to perform in the ecosystem. Some strawberries may be dumber than others, but comparing a strawberry to a human is much, much, more problematic. It's like comparing apples and oranges (pun intended). Without strawberries, or other food, humans would not even exist, therefore the question of intelligence at the species level makes no sense. It only makes sense at the collective level.

The ecosystem functions as one big brain coordinated by the EoT, which is the cumulative intelligence of all lifeforms and processes on Earth. Evaluating the intelligence of an individual life form within this vast network is highly problematic, and only makes sense within a narrative of conflict and competition i.e. who will kill who, first. Looking at intelligence within a single species would be like picking apart a human brain and evaluating each neuron cell separately, to find the most and least intelligent neurons. What makes neuron cells intelligent however, is not who each of them are as an individual entity, but the number and quality of connections with all other cells which they share: their collective intelligence, which belongs not only to them, but to all the other neurons as well. Humanity is just one neuron cell within Earth's brain. This intelligence is shareable, never owned.

Our human-centric and fragmented definition of intelligence can be seen in how both our folklore and scientific disciplines have approached it. We have spent thousands of years asking ourselves whether the dolphin is smarter than the octopus, or if white people are smarter than black people. An intelligent species to us is one that is "problem-solving" in human terms, like a chimp who is able to ask for more bananas by pressing a button, or an octopus able to get itself out of a trap. It is a definition of intelligence which again, is based on conflict and competition, and judged on purely human criteria important to our species, and our species alone. These are incredibly narrow and human-centric definitions of intelligence. We tend to consider a species "intelligent" based on whether it can get itself out of a mess, or how effective it is in killing all the other species in order to dominate, but these are human criteria of intelligence, based on our false narrative of conflict and competition. For us, if the octopus was able to kill every other life form in the ocean and establish an empire, it would become super-intelligent in our eyes. We judge intelligence by human colonialist and supremacist standards, although, ironically, we ourselves are clearly failing to tick the box of "getting out of a mess" by the way in which we have spectacularly failed to address the climate crisis - which we have caused in the first place, because we are of course, incredibly intelligent.

The Fabricated War

Our current existential crisis is nothing but the false narrative of conflict finally coming back to haunt us. We viewed Earth and its species as our enemy for thousands of years, and we have managed to turn it into one. We have started a war where there never was one, ultimately a war with ourselves. What lies at the origin of the climate crisis and ecological overshoot is the false core belief that anything natural outside of the artificial human civilisation is raw, inferior and inherently hostile to us. Perhaps the most shameful of all of our manufactured narratives was the idea that nature was the one who started the war: nature was the "unruly" one, who needed to be tamed. Whether it was a thousand year-old tree cut down or an indigenous tribe exterminated, it was all done under the same principle: they deserved it, because they are "lesser" and "different" life forms. They were not high enough in the intelligence ranking, and therefore in the hierarchy of rights to their existence.

But the false narrative of "advanced civilization vs wilderness" has collapsed. Man was all along the wilderness to be tamed, and nature was the only balanced, sustainable and civilized system that ever existed, uniting all species in harmony and allowing none to dominate over others. Nature was never "out to get us".

Biochauvinism, racism, slavery and colonialism may have set the foundations for today's global economic system, but arguably nothing much has really changed since then. People of color still struggle more than whites for opportunities and economic prosperity. Ball and chain have been replaced by debt slavery across the population, regardless of race. We are all slaves, pinned down like butterflies and compared to each other in an increasingly scrutinizing manner based on our digital trace. The system is constantly creating ever more narratives of conflict, as it tries to open up new sources of revenue. It desperately needs these narratives, if it is to continue.

Yet in principle we are all equal, vital components of the superorganism. All of Earth's 8 million life forms came into existence in the same exact way: out of the dark murk, the silent mud, the restless, nourishing molecular soup that made us all. The soup is now being poisoned by the one species who has forgotten what it is, and where it came from. Only if we demolish the toxic narratives of supremacy, conflict, growth and progress on which we have built this flimsy house of cards, can we develop new narratives upon which a completely new, multi-species social organization can be established. If we ever manage to accept and live by the principle that we are only a fragment of the living ecosystem, it would be the humblest, yet possibly the greatest discovery of mankind. And a game changer in turning around the extinctional spiral we are in.

DECEPTION: THE SHOW MUST GO ON

The Birth of Cakeconomics

Whenever I order a piece of cake at a restaurant, I always wonder how much more cake there is back in the kitchen. Not because I'm greedy, but because it always fascinated me how, from a logistics point of view, the owners of the restaurant manage to achieve that magical goldilocks balance between having plenty of cake for customers on one hand, but not so much cake that it would lead to financial loss due to unsold units, on the other. It must be a headache having to speculate on the level of expected demand, as well as its variations due to low and high-consumption days, or even the shifting demographic profile of the clientele which, I would think, affects which cake flavor they choose, and if they have any desire for cake in the first place. How on earth does any restaurant do this?

As consumers of course, we never have to worry about how the restaurant will magically manage to have our favorite cake slice in stock, if and when we decide to walk into their premises on some random day. How does an entire back kitchen manage to match what is on the menu, at least most of the time? As far as the customer is concerned, the entire menu should be available: thus, when they order, they should be able to select based on their desire, not based on what is best for the restaurant, which would help to reduce waste in the kitchen.

This is pretty much the same principle by which our civilization has been appropriating natural resources: based on its wishes and demands on the day, not based on what is sustainably available in nature. The way we manage our restaurants is a micrography of our global economic model: we have been raiding Earth's kitchen with abandon, in much the same way that we rock up to a restaurant, ordering anything we like just because we happen to have a rectangular piece of plastic in our wallet.

As consumers, and restaurant patrons, we are vital to the survival of this surreal economic system: with each impulsive purchase, we ensure that the system is driven by demand and desire, as opposed to availability and balance. This happens because we are indoctrinated, very early on, with the core values of industrial consumerism: the customer is always right, no product should ever be unavailable, and if something breaks down, fastest solution is to throw it in the trash and buy a brand new identical item immediately. Welcome to cakeconomics.

It is no wonder then why selfishness has reached a peak: hyper-narcissism has been deliberately encouraged and engineered by a psychonomy which recognized, very early on, that selfish and narcissistic people simply buy more stuff. Over decades of "aspirational" marketing, all of us became more and more narcissistic, until this became the norm. This has been great news for the psychonomy, bad news for the planet. As for society itself, it is virtually gone, existing more as a collection of psychonomy-led public services rather than a community. Because of this engineered narcissism, we have all been atomized, separated from each other by layers and layers of algorithm into individual cells within the vast farm we are being reared in. The psychonomy has successfully separated us from each other, so that it can more effectively control us and monetize us, at the individual level. We can all have cake now, but we end up eating it all by ourselves.

Abundance Is An Illusion

An incredibly complex and burdensome system operates behind the cake counter, cleverly hidden from the eyes of the consumatrons. However incredibly complex things may be at the back end, our transactions must appear seamless and easy, so that we have the impression of a faultless, effortless, magical and perpetually stable system which will continue to satisfy all of our demands. But most of all, this deceptively stable system aims to give us the impression that we live in an abundant, magical world where nothing will ever run out, however much we consume. The psychonomic network of goods extraction, manufacturing and supply chains is executed so well, that it literally caters to every need and desire we could have ever had, now available at our fingertips on our computer keyboard. We go to the supermarket and there are dozens of different brands of cereal. It is a perverse, gluttonous fantasy made reality. Surely there must be a catch?

You've guessed it. We have been conned. Our entire economic system is supported by a grand illusion of abundance. This deceptively abundant world that we consider "normal" is actually not sustainable – meaning, it won't be "normal" for very much longer. It is a house of cards, because it does not obey the physics laws of supply and demand that the ecosystem relies upon: in real nature, resources and goods are not abundant. Supermarkets do not exist. Animals have to scavenge for food, and sometimes even skip a meal. Plants agonizingly reach out to the sun, and may need to wait weeks or months for rain. Even human bodies are designed to last without food for days, even weeks. During this time, humans can still function and go about their daily life by metabolizing the fat reserves under their skin. This is our normal way of being, and how we were designed to optimally work. In the real ecosystem resources are scarce, but every being on Earth manages to eat in the end, if they just wait a little bit.

In the normal ecosystem of the planet, consumers are not worshiped and spoiled like gods, as they are today, because this would make the ecosystem go bankrupt within a matter of hours. And this is in fact what is happening: Earth is being raided by humans who live in an illusion of abundance. The illusion of abundance is the dogma behind the most destructive force on the planet: extractive, corrosive, toxic necrocapitalism which is bankrupting Earth and ending life itself.

The dogma "if the consumer wants it, we will bring it to them, whatever it takes", has been fundamental to supporting the illusion of abundance. The consumer became both a victim and a deity: at no point should demand fail to be met, even if this means having to open more sweatshops, slash and burn more forest, or kill the last tuna fish on the planet.

The Fraud That Is Money

The restaurant manager is therefore an illusionist: he may have succeeded in convincing his patrons that everything on the menu is available, but it is all a dirty magic trick. While he maintains smiles on the main floor, back in the kitchen it is carnage: slash and burn agriculture, extinction, resource depletion, just to make some cake. There is a long list of victims and long-term consequences. But we can't stop now. The show must go on. We need to feed the customers. The illusionist must keep the magic trick going for as long as possible, even if the odds are not in his favor. How does he do it?

Through another magic trick: money. Money is abstract, invented currency which does not really represent value. It is an instrument of profit which is able to respond to variations in supply and demand: if consumer demand increases, the price per cake slice just goes up. As more and more people ask for cake, the higher price triggers more production, and everyone wins: the consumer, the restaurant owner, the farmers supplying flour, butter, sugar and eggs. Of course, all of these winners belong to the same species: humanity.

Earth is the big loser: the animal and plant species that participated in making the cake got absolutely nothing out of this process. Some had to be tortured or had to die so that the cake can be made, others even went extinct in the process. An uninsured, undocumented immigrant somewhere in an industrial-sized bakery not far from the restaurant had to break their back making cake batter all day. Untold carbon emissions had to be released to create the steel industrial kitchen machinery he is surrounded by, which consume vast quantities of electricity.

And as for the consumer, when they got to the restaurant they realized that they had some leftover cake in their fridge at home, after all. It turns out they didn't need cake. They just needed to get some fresh air, so they filled up their tank in their steel car to drive to the restaurant and have their cake slice, instead of the one at home, which they will probably throw out as soon as they get back.

The plastic card that they have in their wallet is the consumer's own magic trick. The invention of money has been the single biggest fraud committed against nature. Money is a loan of equity stolen from humanity's one and only lender, Earth, distributed to bored consumatrons driving around in their gas guzzlers for their next cake fix. As with all equity, it becomes worthless when the creditor goes bankrupt. Humanity has maintained the illusion of abundance by committing financial fraud through the invention of money.

The key to all financial fraud is deception. Our civilization has perpetrated its theft against nature by rearing Michelin-starred financial concoctioninsts and illusionists, and an army of Harvard-educated economists proud to be studying an economic system that does not even obey first-grade math: it obeys the illusions of the psychonomy. We are amassing a massive debt towards the animals, plants and the climate system of the planet which we are demolishing, in order to temporarily sustain the impossible illusion of abundance. Colonialism, intensive agriculture, slavery, mining. We have been living on "cake credit" for hundreds if not thousands of years, producing what we need through a process that eventually breaks the cake oven itself, and sets the house on fire. All of us with jobs are being paid by an economic system that is a bankrupt Ponzi scheme, and has actually never turned a real profit at any point in its existence. Our one and only lender, Earth, is going down, and she will be taking us down with her, very soon.

The Invention Of Waste

But there is one last magic trick that the restaurateur-cum-illusionist must perfect: he needs to be able to coordinate a complex, often unpredictable logistical operation from the production line all the way to the table, so that the customer gets their cake at an affordable price, and the illusionist turns a profit no matter what happens. It seems like such an impossible feat, that you would assume the goldilocks balance of supply and demand would only have been achieved if the Harvard-educated economists were having board meetings with the restaurant's manager on a weekly basis, using advanced modelling and predictive analytics of cake consumption data and other variables, and adjusting cake supply accordingly on a daily basis. They would look into the entire cake process and try to make it more energy efficient and profitable, yet fair and sustainable. There would be environmental scientists advising on the impact of overconsumption, population increase and intensive farming on the natural environment, and how this could affect "the future of cake on Earth". There would be a social scientist and immigration advisor helping Julio from Guatemala who works long hours in the cake kitchen, so that he is more valued and appreciated, and better rewarded for his back-breaking work. There would be a doctor helping him with his diabetes, a result of working in cake quality control for years.

Instead, there is a much, much easier magic trick which avoids solving all of the above problems, and increases the restaurant's profit in one single step: throwing all of the unused cake in a new human invention called "the bin". We'll just make more cake, at a cost to workers and natural resources, increase the price per slice to cover for our expenses, and dump whatever cake is left at the end of the day in a place which we will call "trash", which other people can't see. This way the restaurant is always stocked, the customer always gets what they want, and we even make a profit. The illusion of abundance has been saved, for yet another day.

Along with money, the concept of waste is the double-fraud which completes the cycle of extractive, exploitative, self-destructive necrocapitalism. Both money and waste are abstract concepts engineered by humans. In a real ecosystem nothing is ever wasted. Every time uneaten cake is thrown in the restaurant's dumpster, unnecessary work hours in the cake factory have been spent. Plants and animals have been unnecessarily slaughtered. CO_2 was unnecessarily emitted to fire up the oven. We may label the dumped cake as "waste", but it came at an incredible cost to the planet. Waste is yet another illusion.

All magic tricks have to end sooner or later, when the curtain comes down and spectators return to their normal, real lives. Our psychonomy has invented a number of magic tricks to keep the illusion going: abundance, money and waste being just three of them. But there is barely any Earth left to destroy, without completely breaking the cake oven. The show is ending. The red velvet curtain (and the red velvet cake) comes crashing down on the illusionist, taking the ceiling along with it. And that's not his only problem: a starving mob is about to eat him alive.

The self-destructive entity of necrocapitalism will push the entirety of Earth, including humans, to their absolute limits. Maximum profit requires maximum exploitation, and maximum extinction. This, will end in maximum collapse of the ecosystem, and the psychonomy that has been attached to it like a bloodsucking leech.

It takes an incredible amount of effort to kill an entire planet. But rest assured, we have done all we could to achieve this, while maintaining our illusions and delusions. The magician will die on the stage, doing what he always did best. But this one will be his last, magic trick.

WE WERE NEVER IN CONTROL

A Brain Designed To Exploit

Contrary to what our impressive technological milestones and achievements may suggest, the surprising truth is that we have never really been in charge of what happens to us. As a biological organism aiming to maximize its chances of survival, all of our accomplishments and decisions were blindly driven with survival in mind: economic growth, technological evolution, population increase - whatever it takes, at whatever cost to us or to the planet. From our humble beginnings as a monocellular life form and up to today's complex industrial civilization, evolution has never stopped selecting for exactly the same traits in humans: greedy and exploitative tendencies, and the physical and mental skillsets which accompany these - given that, it is these precise skillsets which are the most likely to avert extinction in the short term. These tendencies are what has been in control all this time - and what is still in control today.

Our brain therefore was enlarged and optimized to become a resource exploitation logistical device: it was customized to "mine" all resources within its environment efficiently, quickly, and most importantly, at terrifying scale. When our brains became much bigger, the seemingly quantum leap in data processing power that evolution gifted us with was so immense, that its impact has still not been fully realized today. Despite our lives becoming so much more intellectually demanding within the last few decades, a time frame over which biological evolution can be assumed to have been negligible, our brain has remarkably been able to keep up with any and every new sophisticated technology and lifestyle we developed (just about).

In other words, we manage to do all of the things we do today using the exact same brain that humans several thousands of years ago before us used, living lives much less complex than ours. Those humans would never have imagined that their brain could do all the things it does today. It would seem that we, as crazy as this may sound, are still exploring the limits and capabilities of what is still a relatively new "gadget". We are still uncovering just how much our brain can handle, imagine, envisage, create. And at the same time, this immense brain allows us to continue to make our life even more complex: it allows us to be unbelievable adaptable, and almost reinvent our lifestyle and society every three decades or so, at the current speed.

Greed Eats Wisdom For Breakfast

Yet despite this level of "intelligence", our in-built greed is still the prime, natural driver not just for us, but for any other species, whether it is an amoeba or a Nobel prize winner. However complex and sophisticated our DNA becomes, it will always self-select for genes coding for attributes which favor its successful replication into the future i.e. survival. Social intelligence, philosophy and ethics cannot weed out greed, ever, simply because greed will always be supercharged by the evolutionary process. Therefore, although we often erroneously think of ourselves as the only species with true sentience and "free will" to take our own decisions, the reality is that we have never really been in charge. The most important factor in any of our decisions is, and will always be, our own personal survival in the very short term. This is a permanent, indestructible feature of our hardware which came with our original factory settings: our DNA.

This DNA codes for mental skillsets and hormonal responses which determine, to a large degree, our attitudes and behaviors. These attitudes and behaviours were subsequently further refined and shaped by our environment within different social contexts and timepoints in our history. Different societies had different permutations of these behaviours, which became embedded in local popular culture until they finally began to be referred to as social "norms" and "traditions" of that specific culture. While indeed norms vary from one culture to another, and they may appear on the surface as frivolous variations of costume and cuisine, at their core they are all ultimately driven by the big elephant in the room: the part of our greed and survival instinct which is DNA-based: it simply cannot be tackled.

Europeans may have had an incredibly vast array of languages, costumes and traditions, yet all of them at some point, when conditions were just right, exercised their instinct to invade, colonize, and exploit lands at the far reaches of the world. Other cultures across the world would have done just the same had they had the technological superiority which Europeans had.

Of course, this in-built survival instinct is not good news when it comes to addressing the apocalyptic catastrophe we have in store for this planet. Implementing any of the myriad of already existing solutions for stopping our self-destruction would require us to be able to step outside of the context of economic growth and exploitation, which is so paramount to our identity. We simply lack the faculties to do this, and proof of this is that the more solutions to climate change emerge, and the more conscious our discussions become on what it is that we need to urgently do, the more obstinate our resistance grows towards implementing any of these solutions. Why?

Greed and short-term survival are simply stronger drivers. It could even be argued that our intelligence has regressed as our society became more exploitative and automated - that whatever spiritual, deep, true intelligence humans may have initially possessed, has been overwhelmingly wiped out by the greed-related psychoses which our necrocapitalist system has been selecting for, again and again, over millennia of social and genetic evolution. Our brain was not made to excel in ethics, philosophy and ecology. It evolved to efficiently exploit resources. Undoubtedly, our advanced processing power further supercharged the manner and scale by which we exploited this planet, while at the same time failing to impart in us the wisdom to install our own limits on how, and how much of, these finite resources we used. This was not even part of the discussion. We never even attempted to invest thought into these areas, at least not by enough voices which could resonate with a critical mass of leaders, administrators, or the general public.

Thus, while our brain is able to imagine, create, innovate and think of alternative ways in which society can be organized, ultimately it prefers to stick to familiar scripts which serve its exploitation goals i.e. what it was originally made for: the right here, right now. Subsequent chapters in this book delve deeper into how our brain may have evolved, and provide a theory for our severe cognitive limitations. It is these limitations which are by far our greatest challenge.

Humanity vs. The Ecosystem

It is important to understand the unstoppable growth of our civilisation through the power of the natural exploitation logistical device which is our brain. This brain was, and still is to this day, a frighteningly powerful killing machine. While all species, when given a chance, can exhaust natural resources, only for humans did natural destruction become a global collapse event. There was simply no ecosystem which could recover fast enough from such efficient destructive capacity. We didn't simply limit other species' populations. We made them extinct. Yet this natural exhaustion became an unofficial foundational principle for an entire civilisation, which managed to do something no other species had done: to overcome all natural limits to consumption, as well as all the natural predators that the ecosystem had put in place to keep us in check. From very early on, we completely broke the ecosystem:

it was simply not able to keep up with our destructive capacity. What followed, was the end of everything.

Is Self-Destruction Inevitable?

It could be argued that this was inevitable, and that the process of evolution ultimately always leads to a big collapse: while over the course of millennia the ecosystem may become more and more diverse, it eventually reaches a peak point of diversity where out of so many millions of species, the chances of complex intelligence arising are now very high. All it takes is for just one of these species to become intelligent. Because when this one species ceases to have any serious predators, the eventual destruction of the entire ecosystem is only a matter of time - unless this species becomes self-aware of what it is doing and decides to put the brakes on itself.

Humans are to Earth what the Big Bang is to the universe: the universe grows and grows, until suddenly one day it all goes back to square one, and the story of life and evolution begins from scratch. Unchecked greed, after all, does what it says on the tin: boom and bust, otherwise known as self-destruction.

It doesn't require academic analysis or debate therefore, to conclude that our greedy personal survival instinct is much stronger than any rational solution. Are we introspective enough to recognize this evolutionary trap, rise above it, and begin to cultivate the mental tools we desperately need, despite this self-destructive pre-disposition? It is a question of nature vs. nurture, and nature is overwhelmingly winning thus far, hands down, for the overwhelming duration of our history.

Victims of Evolution

Addressing climate change and the ecological apocalypse is therefore not an issue of yet another technology, or increased brain processing power for that matter. These two approaches have both run their course. It is an issue of truly, genuinely claiming our own destiny, for the very first time in our 200,000 years of existence as modern humans. It is about finally being in control. As critical as this shift in thinking is, it seems impossible, given that much of humanity does not even believe we are responsible for what is happening to this planet. Those who accept no responsibility have already given up on their potential to make a difference in the course of events. They have given up on taking control of their destiny.

It is of course a profound disappointment, not to mention a paradox, that evolution didn't know any better than select for some of the most ecocidal attributes in humans. But evolution is not an infallible process. Its drawback is that it can only operate based on current wisdom, that is, on what it knows at the time of mutation. It is always completely oblivious to the future. We evolved during an era of abundance on the planet, which is not the case today. The human brain was never built to comprehend the possibility of running out of ecosystems to destroy, and species to make extinct. Civilization developed in a womb of abundance and gluttony, ignorant of the very concept of running out of anything.

New evolutionary mutations, new species of humans who think differently, would be needed urgently in this new, depleted environment we have created. But of course this is impossible. The life forms which evolve after we've wrecked Earth, will probably have no choice but to be a bit more thrifty, at least for the first few million years, until overheated Earth finds some balance. As far as humans go, we cannot simply redesign ourselves as if we were a new iphone version. Evolution is a cumulative process, and DNA code can only be amended, not rewritten. We have gone too far down the evolutionary path to remove greed out of our biological system. Crocodiles are much more ecological in comparison: they can go without a meal for 12 months, and don't even get grumpy about it. They have more patience and Zen wisdom than our own Dalai Lama. They have a much better chance of survival, and definitely deserve it much more than us based on their track record.

I know that many philosophers, environmental activists, economists and scientists may find this all too dystopian and defeatist. They may still believe that, we have the power vested in us to take control of our destiny. I wholeheartedly hope that they are right, and that I am very wrong, but I come to this conversation from a biology perspective, and biology eats philosophy, economics and social theory for breakfast any day. Biology is the raw blood and bones of who we really are. Our hormones and our "wiring" do determine much of our behavior, unfortunately.

Our Greed Now Owns Us

Consider today's world. Despite all of this technology and sophisticated civilization, do we really think any of us are in charge of our lives? The same survival instincts still rule at large, the same irresistible "lifeforce" within each organism to greedily appropriate as much resource from its environment as it possibly can.

The difference between humans and other species is that greed for us is as much an instinct, as it is an institutionalized, perennialized and sophisticated economic system which controls every aspect of our daily needs, and every corresponding natural resource catering to these. The irresistible survival instinct which all species have is, in the case of humans, harnessed and monetized by an organized psychonomy which has become impossible to escape, unless one goes off-grid and completely checks out. As an industrial society, we have long ago outsourced our future to this greedy economic system which supersedes any national or global political entity. It is above religion, politics, and society. It is called Business. Human civilization has become a self-destruction machine. We can blame evolution, or we can dare for once to take control of our destiny and dream of a different civilization, and a different outcome. It is up to us to prove that the emergence of intelligent life on this planet was not a tragic mistake of evolution.

The Age of the Farmed Consumatron

What is also unique to our species is that the survival of this economic system has become more important than the survival of humanity. The system only cares about propagating itself, and it does this by farming more humans and creating more consumer needs in order to increase its revenue. Human society did not invent business. It became a business all to itself. The continued cheap mass production of goods necessitated the cheap mass production of consumers within closely monitored, farmed environments called cities. No commercial modern farm can stay financially afloat without maintaining a high cattle headcount. Humans are therefore to this day being farmed by the billions, raised to become identical consumatrons devoid of spiritual consciousness and individuality. We are being bred like sheep inside cheap, hastily constructed jenga towers, waiting for the moment when they come down on us. Meanwhile we are all strongly encouraged, and with the utmost urgency, to keep on consuming, polluting and having more children: not for our benefit, but solely to prevent this toxic, unsustainable capitalist system from collapsing into itself any earlier than it would have anyway. Excess has become a way of life. Most of the things this civilization preoccupies itself with are unnecessary, absurd, and in fact, damaging to the well-being of both humans and the planet. We are on a self-destructive path over which we seem to have, by all sights and sounds, absolutely no control. This is simply an observation, not a fatalistic opinion.

The industrial revolution, institutionalization of society and digital marketing all evolved with the same, common goal: to increase control over humans, ensure that the farm grows bigger, scale up consumption of industrial feed and create easy-to-manage identical human cattle, who all helplessly depend on this system like a hospital patient hypodermically connected to a drip feed. Modern human life is as unnatural as that of a factory chicken, living and dying under electric light. We have relinquished control of our lives long ago to this factory, addicted to its growth hormones, and not knowing any better. Moreover, this system is completely watertight. There is absolutely no escape. The "chicken humans" do not even know where the exit door is and what "free-range" means, growing up in a cultural context which has legitimized an increasingly artificial and complicated life, yet one which feels so vividly real, so deceptively safe and convenient to each and every one of us - given that this is the only reality we have ever known of. But there is a better life out there: outside of the farm.

The system of course has evolved to give us the false impression that we DO have full control and choice over our lives. But this is a make-believe freedom under Big Brother's watch: the list of choices we are being offered is always limited, and the decision options further narrowed down to almost a prescription. They represent different flavors of the same, one option, which aims to maximize returns for an economic system addicted to profit. Sentenced by birth to be stakeholders and at the same time victims of this scheme, we are meticulously miseducated and groomed to become greedy, insatiable consumers, running around all day working, purchasing, paying bills and destroying Earth in the process. Not only have we lost any rudimentary control over our lives, but our own lives simply do not matter anymore. It is the preservation of the hard, cold profit indexes of the economic machine which matter, and which all of us work for. We are the cattle in the farm: we do most of the work munching on processed food to fatten up, yet all we get in the end is to be put up for sale as cheap meat, and ultimately, become terminated as each new batch of consumatrons enters the farm for processing and indoctrination.

This Ponzi scheme of "wealth creation for wealth creation's sake" has been an Armageddon of natural wealth destruction for the planet. Most of us are simply not able to see this, as we are blinded by the "customer rewards system" that has been integral to the success of the psychonomy. As the stakeholders, we thought we were getting something for ourselves out of all this natural destruction. But the rewards are about to turn into losses. Karma will be knocking on our door. It won't matter if you are the cattle, or the farm owner. You're all going down.

All Lifeforms Are Worthless Now

From this dystopian yet pragmatic perspective, human civilization is technically no longer run by humans. It is run by profit and algorithms, both completely selfish, non-human entities which have zero ethics and no social or environmental conscience (arguably we lack these as well). Human life, and all other life for that matter, is therefore rapidly losing value within this matrix. Its only reason to exist is to serve the system, a precarious position to be in: it is quite possibly a matter of time before "the system" of algorithmocracy-infused necrocapitalism eventually crosses a pivotal point of becoming self-sustaining, and realises that it doesn't need humans to continue its journey. Too many overheads.

We have effectively been hijacked and turned into working zombies, simply so that this necrosystem can continue regardless of our own well-being or future. We are now following its plans, not our plan, which has always been nebulous anyway. We are officially "the help". Our psychonomy, increasingly more sentient, operates on the principle of putting profits above people and nature. The cheaper the labour and the more agressive the natural destruction, the better the profit margin looks. The workforce is always a workhorse: dependable, yet expendable. And just like true zombies, we have no idea that we have already been rendered technically obsolete by this very system which we created in the first place. We have made ourselves disposable, in the most perverse, self-destructive and unconscious way.

Is There An Alternative to Self-Destruction?

This system would have made sense to an extent, if at least it represented a sustainable economic model which could continue into the future, with or without us. It could have perhaps at least secured our survival within a mutually parasitic/symbiotic relationship between human and machine. But it isn't sustainable, as it is based on the exponential leveraging and eventual destruction of the very resources which it uses. It is exhausting its own fuel, and it does so at an accelerating pace, much like stock market derivative instruments built out of fake money. As it currently stands, this system is made to self-destruct. Not because it is stupid, but because we have programmed our own self-destructiveness into it. Given its emerging super-intelligence, it will have options to consider for its future, whether this future includes humans or not. Sadly, little of this, if any, will be up to humans to decide.

For the time being, all of Earth, including its beings, resources, climate systems and all of humanity, is being parasitically exploited by a non-human, semi-sentient, self-destructive Ponzi scheme entity. We shallowly call this system "capitalism", not understanding that we have given it free reign to the point where it owns us in ever so many ways, while it cleverly tries to convince us that we are all free. It is already in full control of our lives, and of the planet's resources. We are all parts of a psychonomic machine which is designed to eventually eat itself, down to the very last, dried-up remnants of its carcass. Yet somehow, this thing can stay in a zombified state as it waits for its next opportunity for investment to appear. It is possible that one day, it may realise its own vicious self-destructive cycle.

The terrifying truth very few realize is that capitalism, in its current iteration, has no owners anymore. There is no "off" switch and no driver at the wheel of this automated train to hell, because this Thing now owns us instead. It will drive this planet to its inevitable, uninhabitable next chapter. By the way things are unfolding, it looks like a sure death sentence for human civilization as we have come to know it, a dead end for a large proportion of biological life, and, depending how bad things get, a significant hurdle for any new complex life forms who may try to emerge one day, out of the planet's radioactive ashes. The planet will be entering a completely new chapter, both as a climate and as an ecosystem - the latter one possibly consisting of more sustainable, digital versions of the previous biological iterations.

Whatever the outcome, human parasitism on Earth has already become too efficient for its own sustenance. The system is already beginning to crash. For the first time in our history, all civilizations will begin to decline simultaneously, part of a worldwide systemic collapse and a possible end to the human chapter altogether, given the reality of the inhabitable new temperatures in the majority of the planet's surface. A new climate and completely new post-Anthropocene era will begin on a completely new planet: one with its own new climate conditions, ocean currents, and possibly new primordial ecosystems eventually rising out of the plastic debris, radioactivity, and heat. These new biological life forms will likely be competing with the digital, non-DNA-based descendants of ourselves we've left behind.

We abandoned all 8 million other species of this planet when we signed under the dotted line to join the ranks of this Ponzi scheme, forgetting that we, are one of these 8 million species. The profit numbers and stock prices may continue to look good for a while, just as we become poorer and poorer and the system tries to tell us via its clever, algorithm-driven propaganda that everything is fine. But soon, we will be finding ourselves having to steal from each other in this oversubscribed, collapsing betting scheme. We, collectively the stakeholders of this self-destructive corporation, will pay the full price. As for the "system" itself, it is already non-biological, and will possibly hibernate until the next resource it manages to hitch a ride with - whether that resource is a being, a mineral, or an energy source.

OUR GAME-ENDING LOVE
AFFAIR WITH TECHNOLOGY

Love at First Sight

Despite their impressive momentum and efficiency, all of our civilizations have been incredibly naïve when it came to envisioning their long term future. There was always creative food for thought, and plenty of incentive in planning for the immediate next day. However, little of the decision-making was sensible from a longer term perspective. When it came to tackling the bigger long-term questions, it was as if the future didn't even exist. Our approach has always been tactical at best: focusing on short-term gains, while completely ignoring the bigger, long-term existential challenges. There was far more interest in achieving immediate yet temporary progress, than in ensuring the conditions were met which could sustain that progress in the long term.

For this reason, the emphasis has always been a technological one: it was the technological tools which provided us, and still do, with the fastest and most spectacular bursts of growth, and which bring about an almost immediate social transformation, every single time.

We quickly learned that technology was viral, it was a profit maker, and for these reasons, virtually unstoppable. Very early on we almost resigned ourselves, sat back and watched as technological viruses ravaged through our civilizations like wildfires in the night. In this chapter, I will develop an opinion on what this has cost us, and how we tragically relinquished three things to machines: our freedom, our happiness, and our own responsibility. I will explain why this happened, and what the existential repercussions are as we continue down this path, full speed.

Love is Blind

We surrendered to technology a long time ago. Along with personal gain, it was internalized defeatism towards the inevitability of technology which prevented leaders and planners from thinking more carefully about the impacts of technological change: to contemplate how humans felt, at the individual level, experiencing and living in these new, magical worlds that had been constructed for them. Convincing ourselves that every new innovation would be an improvement, we never conducted any risk analysis. Perhaps there wasn't even time to think, as we were all too busy getting used to the changes that each new technological whiplash brought on our doorstep, piling upon still fresh wounds from the previous technological revolutions.

Perhaps we were simply too much in love: we never wanted to entertain the thought that the object of our affection, technology, could be hiding something so sinister underneath. We accepted our dysfunctional relationship, we accepted the domestic violence, in exchange for the safety and security that technology promised us. At every step of our technological journey, we forgot to ask the most important questions: Was this progress? Was this really what we wanted? Is this where we want our children to grow up? Who are we? What are we? And where the hell are we going?

But the deeper, and most disturbing question we forgot to ask, and which remains unanswered today, is: were we the ones consciously transforming our lives, or was technology transforming us instead? Were we in control of this process, or were these technological viruses in the driver seat, infecting our society, leaving us barely capable of mustering a response while we still processed the shocks of each technological revolution that had just passed?

So many technological innovations are conceived and designed with the original promise of bringing people closer. But they end up taking up so much physical and mental space, that the opposite is often observed. They become huge objects separating people and fragmenting societies. Given that with each new technology the focus of our attention becomes an increasingly complex and transactional life, we forget the most important thing: each other. We end up giving up all of our friends, so that we can focus on our lover: technology.

There must have come a point when technological innovation speeded up so much that, people realised they had no choice but to accept, to have to put up with, big and rapid changes which would likely happen during their own lifetime. They just gave up trying to resist, and decided that they would simply have to mold their new life, their entire existence, however best they could, around each new technological monolith that ushered itself into their lives.

Had we been violently pushed aside? Were we not in charge anymore? Had humans simply become vehicles for technology's expansion and evolution? And most importantly, had we become something lesser and inferior, perhaps outdated, given that technology mutates and evolves much, much faster than us?

A Co-Dependent Relationship

These are all very valid questions, which we should be asking retrospectively, all in the context of a bigger question from a practical and biological perspective: how does a human, essentially an animal that does not physically change over time (especially now that medicine has virtually halted natural selection and therefore evolution), cope in a rapidly changing environment? While in nature species which experience such extreme changes go extinct very quickly, humans had managed to survive, forming a co-dependent relationship with technology based on mutual abuse, and mutual tolerance.

But how was our mental and physical health affected? Were our new societies (now largely run by technology) beneficial to the individual? Or was this abusive relationship inflicting and internalizing trauma upon trauma? For example, while today we may have significantly increased our life span, how meaningful are these new, long, lives we are living?

Given that innovation always moves at breakneck speed, there is never the time, or even the desire, to test the effects of new technologies on our well-being. Any caution is silenced by excitement. From cigarette smoking to pesticides to artificial intelligence, humanity has always learned the hard way which of these innovations are good for us, and which will simply need to be tolerated. Civilization has always been an ongoing experiment, and we are the mad scientists: too risk-taking to stop and think, and always willing to be guinea pigs in our own experiment.

A Path of Self-Rejection

Had we been too quick to roll out the red carpet for technology, passively accepting all of the conveniences it had bribed us with, for the price of saying goodbye, forever, to essential parts of our "human", biological being? Like a patient waking up in an operating theatre, wondering whether all of their parts are still in place, we found ourselves one morning changed, modified, "adjusted", to fit into our new prosthetic life. We suddenly felt some of our parts had gone missing. But we didn't even know which ones, because we couldn't remember anything. It was too late. Everything fit together like a glove, but it still didn't feel right. It wasn't the same. We were not ourselves anymore. We had become something else, altogether.

However much technology surrounds us and supports us, deep inside we are still made out of flesh, blood, emotions and dreams. Yet each successive technological virus appears to bypass our most "human" needs, at best adjusting itself to any severe side-effects it may have had on its host humans, who end up embracing the virus while at the same time numbing themselves to any internal alarms. Putting aside the dazzling array of consumeristic and other benefits we reaped through technology, are we actually happier than the generations before us? Or have we sacrificed too much of ourselves? Is the patient having post-operative regrets?

Today these questions remain unanswered, as technological evolution accelerates and reaches breakneck speed, leaving us to eat dust while it disappears into the distance. Yet we have completely embraced what is happening to us, maybe because many of us feel there is nothing to do but accept it, or maybe because we cannot even fathom ourselves outside of the context of technology anymore. It is easy to make the argument that we have been demoted, turned into a peripheral hardware accessory within a much more efficient, emerging non-DNA-based AI civilization. Is this the beginning of the end? Have we succumbed already?

It is easy to look at this situation and concur that it is already way too late for us to go back to feeling more human, feeling like ourselves. We have arguably become too tech-dependent. But as long as humans are a species made of flesh, blood, emotions and dreams, they will have needs which are very different to those of machines. We are not machines, and this is precisely the mistake we have been making: comparing ourselves to them, in the same way that a lover often wants to become like the person they are in love with. Many of us are desperate to become machines: efficient, productive, multitasking superhumans who never blink an eye. The corporate world is full of unhealthy stereotypes of what a successful professional is, using criteria much more applicable to machines than humans.

In order to understand what is happening to us and answer all of these questions, it is important to go back to the beginning of events, and realize that we have been enmeshed in a toxic, unconditional love affair with technology which started millennia ago. In a fashion typical to that of any blind, lovestruck human, we have given ourselves an inferiority complex towards the object of our affection.

Our civilization has an inadequacy complex against machines, which is about to worsen as AI approaches and surpasses us. In the same way that we rejected, and subsequently destroyed, natural "wilderness", we are beginning to reject anything "non-machine-like" about us. We want to become more and more like the non-human entity we are in love with. This is a dangerous moment in our history, and the wrong path for us - because again, at a fundamental level, we are not machines. Not yet.

Trading Freedom for Progress

This co-dependent love affair explains how the temptation for humanity to succumb, and submit to technology unconditionally, was too much to resist. Our freedom was the first to be given up, as we trusted technology with our life. Facing the unknown with vacant, unjustified optimism, we quickly replaced our insecurities and uncertainties about ourselves with the comforting dogma that technology was "loving us back": it was working for us, when in fact it had almost domesticated us for its own benefit. Our adoration of technology, not simply as a means to an end, but as the ideal ultimate destination for humanity's evolution, continued through the ages as we looked down upon our "human errors" and "inadequacies", and we looked up to a day when there would be more machines to help us. Driven by blind adoration, we nurtured the expectation that this inanimate entity will be forever by our side (and on our side), and that one day it may even solve all of our existential problems, including the climate crisis. This belief has been incredibly naïve, and may likely prove to be catastrophic.

But it was too late already. We were too corrupted by the technological goodie bag that arrived, every time a new innovation entered our lives. Beware of geeks bearing gifts. Technology was the Trojan horse that was enough to glaze over our eyes and tempt us with lazy, easy gains. The price? Auctioning off the last remaining pieces of ourselves to an increasingly sentient entity that does not represent the interests of the human species, simply because it isn't even human. It is a machine, and just like us, it only cares about itself. By putting all of our faith and trust in technology, we had relinquished a substantial part of our freedom. And yes, we did become something "lesser", but only because deep down we believed that we were lesser.

Happiness, Outsourced

Along with relinquishing our freedom, we gave up on the notion of true happiness, replacing it with counterfeit versions which only made sense in a machine world: we started quantifying happiness based on the number of consumer goods we buy and on GDP, rather than on having a meaningful existence, exactly because we increasingly became like machines: focusing only on the numbers, and the quantities of things. Today, we are as far as we have ever been from answering the question "are we happy?", for a very simple reason: we keep trying to answer the question in machine terms, not human terms, forgetting first and foremost that we had originally come into this world already happy, a long, long time ago.

Happiness is not attained but experienced. It is something that you awaken to, rather than travel towards. Today happiness is an artificial human construct, based on greed and insecurity. The more one tries to define happiness, the more unhappy they become. This is because happiness has been exploited and weaponized by a psychonomy which tried to turn it into a checklist of products, careers and "life steps" which only serve the necrocapitalist matrix. But the more one tries to follow this ridiculous checklist, the longer it becomes. Happiness is not a recipe, a list, or a doctor's prescription. Happiness is a completely personal, unique and individual issue which each of us needs to pursue and explore on their own, distanced from any advice, instruction or marketing mantra. This is becoming impossible in a world where our range of choices is becoming ever more narrow, and the choices themselves increasingly prescriptive. It is nearly impossible to see through the fog of greed, when the fog has become the norm. We have been turned into narcissistic consumatrons, rewarded for the most selfish actions by a system which desperately wants to self-destruct.

Atomized and Identical

Happiness therefore can only be genuine, and technology has played a huge part in making us unhappy, by setting all kinds of milestones, expectations and consumeristic ideals about what a happy human looks like, applied through a blanket approach to all of us, when actually each human is unique and happy with very different things.

We naturally evolved to be very different from each other as individuals, so that when we come together as a society we complement each other's skills. Now that our mechanised psychonomy is turning us all into the same person, we are becoming incompatible with each other, as well as distanced from our true selves. The more alienated we become from each other and from ourselves, the more we will turn to technology to "complete us": as the only safe, reliable shoulder to lean on. Technology is already merging into us: not physically yet, but mentally. And in doing so, it is literally ripping apart our society as we had come to know it - one human at a time.

A Human Problem

But happiness is a question that our technologies and machines do not have to worry about. Happiness, and human happiness for that matter, is not their problem. Happiness is exclusively a human problem. Machines don't have the emotions, feelings of isolation and social needs that we have, and if they do develop these someday, they will be on a separate cosmos of social hierarchy with its own rules and needs which will be very different from ours.

Yet despite this, we have sought to rationalize, simplify, and automate happiness, reducing it down to digital code which our machine friends can estimate, calculate, and extrapolate. We have chosen to increasingly mechanize and automate so much of what makes us intrinsically human. This perversion appears to have no end in sight. We have stiflingly surrounded ourselves with layer upon layer of digital paraphernalia, naively assuming that the little human buried somewhere within this new ecosystem of machines would still remain "human". We emotionally maimed ourselves in this impossible quest to emulate machines: to become beings that do not need feelings, do not need genuine, complicated, messy happiness anymore: instead, they will settle for an pre-prescribed, accessible, stale and significantly inferior version of happiness which follows an easy algorithmic formula. Even psychotherapy is going digital.

We have quite irresponsibly outsourced our happiness and the future of this planet to a techno-economic entity which not only does not understand what genuine happiness is, but it doesn't fundamentally have a need for it. Let that one sink in.

Disconnected and Dismembered

Our insight and curiosity into ourselves has been running at a pace much slower than the pace by which we adopt and merge with technology. Technology has, become the false window that we try to see ourselves through now. This filtered reality can only further disorient us. But we have long ago resorted to assuming impact position, passively accepting the social, emotional and existential whiplash of progress. There is never enough inquiry about how we, humans, feel in our new world, surrounded by machines, in an ecosphere infused with new "forever" chemicals which we invented long ago, the impact of which on the human body we still do not know, decades later.

It is no wonder then that the modern human often feels so alienated, disconnected, and many times completely lost. This is the typical symptom in all patients with trauma. The recurring trauma of successive technological impacts has left its mark on humanity, who has done its best each time to lick its wounds and adapt by trying to catch up with the machines, rather than slow down their onslaught. This is a pattern of self-harm reminiscent of repeat co-dependent relationships: the victim attempts to deal with the original trauma by "going back for more", going into another bad relationship with another abusive partner, inflicting upon themselves more and more trauma each time. As they do this, they sink further and further into desperation, inventing an evolving increasingly more toxic coping strategies and addictions.

Dereliction of Duty

The third and most troubling aspect which humans have relinquished to machines is responsibility. We decided to trust machines with so much of our life. But the hope that technology would save us was misguided, given that technology only cares about itself. It also doesn't care about clean air, water, or habitable conditions for fragile, DNA-based life forms like us. Despite this, we placed much of our trust and hope in the promise of technology, along with the responsibility for cleaning up our own messes. We can only resume our responsibility towards ourselves and towards this planet if we own up to the fact that we are, and have always been, the one and only master of our destiny. We are responsible for whatever happens to us, we are not the teenagers anymore. We seem to have relinquished responsibility for our fate and our future, into the collective unconsciousness of our technology-driven society - where this responsibility is abducted by the algorithms of profit and efficiency. We decided to become abducted by technology, once we realised that saving ourselves was too much of a task. As long as this civilization continues to completely surrender to technology, it will continue to fall victim of its own irresponsibility.

Illusions of Progress

Technology-lovestruck humans have always nurtured millennia-old, romanticized, bold yet naive delusions about what their distant future may look like - even as they struggled to concentrate on planning and predicting the immediate next 2-5 years. The default perception always seemed to be that progress is a self-propelled, self-funded locomotive which one simply hangs on to. It was also assumed that the locomotive always moves in the forward direction, and never stalls. This often led to dangerous delusions of progress, even at times when we were actually regressing - delusions which have come with tragic consequences for both human society and the planet. Yet each new generation of humans was reared with the same, de facto mantra: this is the best generation ever, and it is better off than all generations which have come before: better health, better well-being, more happiness. But even these measures are beginning to reverse, with the first data from the United States confirming that population longevity is now beginning to decline.

While "progress" may be true when looking at some of the macroeconomic, quantitative data, it is safe to say that we are beginning to fail in critical aspects which are not measured through our machine-made statistics and indexes. Our quality of life is diminishing, and this is evident in the large parts of our economy which are now dedicated to finding ways of managing, and healing, the many physical and spiritual ailments we have sustained in the name of progress and technology.

The Chain of Farms

Almost every single technological milestone of our past comes with its own very serious caveats, counterarguments, and asterisks. Take food production for example: today's obesity epidemic is the direct result of the incredible progress which took place within our food industry, over the course of just a few decades. While there was tremendous technological advancement in prolonging the shelf-life of what we ate, this often came at a price of markedly decreased nutritional quality, and a complete disregard for long-term health implications. Much of our food became highly addictive industrial feed, almost overnight: loaded with dangerous chemicals, high glycemic index ingredients, and levels of fat, sugar and salt which are completely unnatural for the human body and which in fact humanity had never been exposed to at any point during hundreds of thousands of years of evolution.

As with many other economic processes disrupted by the industrial revolution, our food production underwent a radical shift in focus: the supply and stockpiling of massive quantities of food was prioritized over nutritional quality, and against the once sustainable, ecologically viable methods of production which used to be the norm. As necrocapitalism, cakeconomics and supermarketization progressively seized ownership of the entirety of the "farm-to-table" process, the objective of food production shifted from feeding humans to making more, and bigger ones, inside the consumatron farms. The goal wasn't food anymore. It was the maximization of consumption. What had once been an essential human need, food, had now become exclusively a business.

All of this of course was perpetrated in the altar of profit, simply to boost the manufacturers' sales margins. It was all about hitting the big financial figures, and what better way to do it than literally make your customers bigger, hungrier, and trapped in life-threatening food addictions - for which of course, they received all the blame and all of the stigma. The manufacturers just received the cash.

Of course, in order to feed all of this proliferating human cattle, we had to create even more farms: consisting of all types of subjugated animals reared under abhorrent conditions, and converted into food objects within the necrocapitalist exploitation matrix. These animals in turn, were fed by the intensive agriculture of monoculture crops grown in endless expanses of ecologically sterile and degraded soils, which had been rendered toxic to all wildlife. We may think that we are the only species who is free, who is on top, and in charge of this whole production process and the food cycle itself. But as a matter of fact, we are merely one farm within a long series of interconnected industrial farms, all chained to each other as part of a choreography of mutual abuse coordinated by the psychonomy. Every ring in the farm chain is another exploitation tragedy. Every growth hormone, piece of microplastic or pesticide, passes from one farm to the next, eventually contaminating the entire chain. The real food chain is owned and operated by Earth. However much humans try to compartmentalise their food production into individual farmed systems, these will always find ways to communicate with each other via the EoT. Whatever we do to our food supply will come back and haunt us.

Equally impressive technological progress and innovation in the industries of marketing and advertizing enabled this new model of gigantic-scale food production to flourish, by boosting demand. Clever, misleading and manipulative advertising campaigns catapulted sales of this overprocessed food, making junk and snack food a staple on the family dinner table, and setting the consumatrons firmly on a path to diabetes, obesity and cancer from the very first days that they come into existence on the planet.

Technological Mummies

But perhaps the most stark example of our maladjustment to technology is how our physical and mental health have responded to the frenetic, complicated lifestyle that the psychonomy has meticulously woven around us, like a suffocating cocoon of layer upon layer of technological strings. Our mental wellbeing has been going into reverse for a long time now, just as we became inseparable from technology, and dependent on it for even the most minor of needs. The bottom line is that we have many more ailments today, as well as more things to worry about. We may live longer, but this is due to technologies and medicines which address modern diseases, some of which did not even exist until recently, and are the direct products of modern technological life. The deep irony, which is indicative of the trap we have set ourselves, is that we keep developing technologies to fix all the traumas we have sustained because of technology in the first place. The madness worsens, just as the cocoon's technological threads get tighter and tighter, leaving us little room to move.

The current mental health state of society already answers the question raised earlier: "will humans be happy in this future world?" There are record levels of depression and anxiety, which most of us accept as necessary, falsely benign compromises of living in, and being part of the psychonomy. We have blindly accepted that in this new, polluted and mechanised world, we are meant to be forever busy, stressed, sleepless, and unhappy. Yet we don't recognize that this is not an ordinary unhappiness. It is a deep existential crisis which has come here to stay, ever since we said goodbye to a life that was much less suffocated by technology. Ever since we relinquished our freedom, our happiness, and our responsibility. Without thinking twice, in our rush to achieve each next milestone in our civilization we galloped forwards, leaving behind both body and soul.

The Convenience Paradox

Much of the objective of technological evolution has been to simply improve on existing processes: making them easier, faster, and less dependent on other humans. While this has been tremendously helpful, it led to the delusion that this increased convenience is really all that our future destiny of happiness is comprised of - completely ignoring the impacts on our emotional world and social psyche. Increasingly adopting machine-defined as opposed to human-defined measures of happiness, we naively assumed that we would be happier, and more fulfilled, in a world that was simply more functional and efficient. Our concepts of progress increasingly focused on boosting our everyday convenience and efficiency, rather than developing our overall well-being.

Working For The Farm

Today, we have already left such a big part of our human side behind, that sometimes it seems we are all working for this invisible technology slavemaster who runs society, rather than working for ourselves and our personal growth. If people in their 20s are already confessing that they don't want to work anymore, it should be an indication of how fake, unsatisfying, abusive and bankrupt our failing corporate civilisation has become. A big part of our work has moved from real, meaningful jobs to so-called "bullshit jobs" whose only purpose is to serve the psychonomic monster we have created. We have moved from making stuff to handling stuff, and from doing to re-doing. We may have built machines to automate our lives, but we became machines ourselves in the process. Work is grossly overrated, and much of it is unproductive and harmful both to the employee and the recipient of services. Many of our jobs involve simply "pushing paper" and pushing CO_2 around the globe.

Even our natural biological rhythms have been sacrificed in order to cater to this system: the sleeplessness epidemic has extended our work hours, increased our energy bills, decreased our life span and damaged the planet's climate. And despite spending more time than ever before in our history being physically awake, we are more mentally and morally unconscious than we have ever been.

It would seem that work itself has lost its meaning for many humans. Unlike machines, humans love to work not only for efficiency, but because they enjoy the process of creativity itself, and have an emotional connection with their work and the fellow humans they serve. This has been lost in many types of work today. Our mechanized work is increasingly unable to provide humans with vital elements of job satisfaction - work and life balance being a key aspect. We all deserve much, much better than this.

Farm Education

In order to cater to this new dystopian framework for work, our mechanised and commercialized educational system had to focus on developing workers, rather than developing humans. It prioritized developing specialized humans with "skills" and "qualifications", rather than whole ones with a world view, critical thinking, a moral compass and a conscience. The latter assets have little to no use in the modern psychonomy, and are in fact, more often than not, a threat to the very existence of the farm. Humans who focus on their personal growth and wellbeing tend to represent an additional cost to employers. Even formerly independent academic institutions are now run as profit-making businesses. Students are treated as consumatrons, paying an exorbitant fee to purchase a diploma which will get them through to the next stage, becoming slaves to the psychonomy before they have even had a chance to join the dystopian madhouse of modern work.

The Distraction Economy

From big corporations to governments and academic institutions, our profit-driven system prefers to render us consciously unconscious, so that we diligently go through the motions of a mechanical existence without stopping to ask the inconvenient questions. Most of us are kept saturated with work so that we have an abundance of tasks on our plate which service the psychonomy, leaving little to no time available to find any personal meaning or purpose, let alone question this entire lifestyle.

Without a sense of personal meaning, or the freedom to pursue our own purpose, it is no wonder that we are beginning to look increasingly similar to each other, as if we are industrial products ourselves. Just like the cheap, mass-manufactured products that they created, humans have become more single-layered, predictable and plastic than ever. Society has become a factory aiming to churn out almost identical humanoids, whose only destiny will be to consume more, think less, and never dare stray away from the assembly line or they risk being quickly dumped into the "unsellable" bin. We have become the sweatshop-made, barcoded, budget versions of our former selves. Our worth is pre-set, our whereabouts are known at all times, and our use-by-date is clearly indicated on the label in the back of our packet. The time is already upon us when we are beginning to question whether we have become capitalist algorithms, just as the algorithms, quite ironically, are wondering whether they have become fully human yet.

Watered-Down Humanoids

It is easy to see the damage that our love affair with technology has inflicted upon us in as little as one generation. The conversations I have with my mother about her childhood are the most enlightening. In my mother's house, there was no fridge. Families in her village would typically prepare their own food and find ingenious ways of storing and preserving it. People were very poor, but tremendous fulfillment came from being connected to the food production process. I remember my mother's story about making home-made pasta, using locally sourced flour, butter and eggs which of course have a much higher nutritional content. After the dough was made, sheets and strings of pasta dough were suspended from every piece of furniture in the house in order to air-dry, before it was to be cut to pieces and stored for the winter. The entire family was involved in the production, and my mother's main role as a little girl was to make sure the cats were kept from jumping on the strings of pasta hanging around the house as it dried. The food was more nutritious, and the family was making memories, feeling connected with each other, feeling grateful to the mill that gave them the flour, the hens in the back yard that laid the eggs, the generosity of nature and the community they lived in. These were happy, fulfilled people, despite their poverty.

Compare this to the five seconds it takes to grab a stale imported packet of bleached pasta from the supermarket shelf, throw it in the trolley and pay for it at the automated check-out which voices the same exact pre-recorded "thank you" every time, coming out of an invisible hole somewhere behind the screen.

It is no surprise that so many of us are wondering whether we are happy, whether we are even alive, given that so much of our life seems to have become a virtual, out-of-body experience. This digital, online life has asserted its own importance, to the point where it dominates over real life. We are becoming algorithmic versions of ourselves, trying to navigate a world which is not simply just another step change, but a massive leap into the unknown. Our friends, our workplaces, our leisurely activities increasingly feel like out-of-body experiences that we are not really living, but experiencing second-hand through our half-asleep avatar. Our human, physical animal has effectively been decommissioned. We are becoming the simplified, watered-down humanoids that the psychonomy wanted all along.

Can our mental and physical health handle this? Many of us are feeling lost and oppressed in such a world. There is increasing pressure to conform to stereotypes propagated by the metaverse, projected on to us by a psychonomy whose only interest is to turn us into efficient consumatrons. In the name of living up to our online avatar and the perfect consumatron we are expected to be, we are increasingly encouraged to compromise, but also "edit", our personal data - anything about us that makes us look different and stand out. At the same time that voices for equality on all fronts are getting louder, racism and other forms of discrimination are taking on much more covert, sinister, digital incarnations, escaping detection

Multiple Avatar Psychosis

The splitting of our personality between the real and the virtual is a recipe for developing almost every form of mental health pathology that exists. The more we divide ourselves into distinct, sometimes incompatible personalities e.g. between our professional and personal avatars, the more difficult it becomes to feel whole, genuine and content at any given occasion. By living our life changing one skin after another to suit whatever role the psychonomy wants us to play, we become imposters. We are never whole, as we always have to hide some aspect of ourselves to please others. Enduring this fragmented state for years, it is no surprise that the longer we participate in this pantomime puppetry of the psychonomic circus, the more we begin to lose sight of who we are. Our real self, our soul, was long ago surgically excised by the psychonomy and replaced by a pre-programmed, implanted script which aims to maximize our contributions as obedient consumatrons within the necrocapitalist matrix. Those of us who have had enough, at some point may embark on a belated, desperate quest to "find themselves" and become whole again. This can be challenging, when so much of who we are as adults has been molded by the psychonomy, while at the same time our most genuine and intrinsically personal traits have either been silenced or erased.

It is no wonder then that an entire industry of life coaching has been set up to monetize our new insecurities in this environment, along with a pathological blogging and social media culture aimed at convincing people that they are not good enough, both physically and mentally, so that they will purchase "life-yoga" solutions and meaningless merchandise. This is the capitalist system acting up yet again, this time to "heal" us, for a fee of course. The same system which damages us, will try to make a profit out of "fixing" us. The psychonomy will always try to drag us back in, just as we try to escape it. Many of us will look for their "real selves" in all the wrong places: a new meaningless and exploitative job, or somewhere in the dark digital metaverse where they will adopt even more avatar personalities. Necrocapitalism is great at applying bandage upon bandage on its unprocessed trauma, rather than bravely looking under the bandage and taking stock of what is happening.

As the world approaches its inevitable collapse and our traumas become more and more evident, the same corrupt system which broke us is now monetizing the industry of "fixing" us. And it does so increasingly without even the involvement of fellow humans. We are sinking deeper and deeper into technological substitutes for our human relationships and the traditional ways of helping each other, as many social services formerly provided by humans to humans have now become "apps". No dystopian novel could have predicted that we would reach this point, this soon.

Planetary Psychosis

Modern civilization is looking increasingly like botched plastic surgery: we went in for a huge facelift job so that we can look great on the outside, without ever asking about the internal complications in the medium term. Rather than stepping back and considering our current position, we are adding one plastic surgery after another, one technological fix on top of the previous technological mistake. It is to be expected that the more our inner world and our relationships are disrupted by technology, the more extreme, bizarre and self-harming our psychological coping strategies are bound to become . We are a threat to the health of this planet, due to our own increasingly unstable mental health.

Our tech-driven psychonomies and our psychotic technologies have been venting our mental illnesses out on Earth, for millenia now. We have been mindlessly destroying our natural heritage in order to fuel consumption and other addictions. The more we try to distract ourselves from our own psychoses, the more they deteriorate - and as they do, ironically, the more monetizable they become by our psychonomic system. In a world driven by money, many of us accept high-paying careers which lead to burnout, isolation and dehumanisation as we succumb to the consumatron lifestyle. There is much unnecessary "ambition" in our world, which is a euphemism for greed and power. But both greed and power are psychoses which only worsen with time. We are driving both ourselves and the planet's climate mad, literally for nothing. And yet, we choose to call all of this "progress". Our toxic love affair with technology continues, unabated.

THE LIMITATIONS OF HUMAN INTELLIGENCE

50 Flavors of Stupid

I hope you're not offended that I've just questioned your intelligence. But this is precisely the same question which Greta Thunberg has been asking the adults of this planet, ever since she was a child: "Can't you look at the figures? Are you blind? What is the matter with you?". Greta had to become an adult herself while she waited for a response to her question, which remains unanswered. Silence speaks volumes, and we now know that we are...well, stupid. But which exact flavor of stupid are we?

As I try to answer Greta's question from the perspective of a biologist, I won't bore you with the obvious about why the world is not banding together: corruption, vested interests, fear of rocking the boat, fear of rocking the almighty CO2 machine of necrocapitalism which pays all our salaries. We all know this, and it is becoming fairly evident that our economic system was not made for Earth, or any planet for that matter. It simply doesn't obey physics. This system could only work as a video game where there are infinite chances to reach Game Over and start again, with a fresh new planet each time. Sadly, we do not have the luxury of a planet B, or C, or D. And this is not a video game.

But where did it all go wrong with our thinking process? This chapter is about our actual brain. And the quick answer to the question "why are we stupid" is two-fold: it's part stupid, part asleep. Just think of a sleeping and stupid person walking down the street. Hold that frightening image for a minute, while we dig deeper.

Tragically False Sense Of Stability

Our brains tend to always want to believe in stability - that is, in an unchanging world. In fact, our brains are obsessed with stability. The concept of things remaining the same is fundamental to our feeling of safety, so that we can "keep calm and carry on" as they say. Even when things are changing fast, our default belief seems to be that nothing much has fundamentally changed. This appears to be a universal thinking pattern which overrides our critical thinking and processing, as evidenced by our historical response to disasters - even when there was ample time to prepare.

Obstinately insisting against all evidence that the world doesn't change, and cannot change, is a deep-rooted attitude which lies at the core of denial for a great proportion of humans. It doesn't matter how educated a person is, this obsession with stability is so strong that it would appear to be part of our brain's hardware.

Denial and ignorance of course, can come with significant benefits. Believing in stability against all presented evidence is associated historically with huge economic and political profit in the short term, despite the long-term catastrophic repercussions. Given that the objective of this false inertia is usually to maintain the economic and political status quo, it is the ruling classes who benefit the most from it. And given that, it is the ruling classes who control much of the media, undoubtedly denial and ignorance have a strong driver to supercharge and propagate themselves in society. Truth has always had a much more difficult time to reach the surface, especially when it is inconvenient.

Additionally, most of our brains are extremely talented in rejecting harsh truths which disturb our comfort, as a way for us to draw courage. Being able to ignore the truth, ignore the paralysing fear and bravely walk into the apocalyptic inferno, is in many ways a valid survival mechanism, and so far in our history this irrational thinking pattern has done wonders for us, allowing us to take risks which otherwise we would never have taken. If we had not taken those irrational risks, our civilisation would look drastically different today.

On the flip side, seeing this pattern of thinking play out in practice is alarming to say the least: however much scientific, factual and rational evidence is put in front of us, we still refuse to believe in scenarios for which we have no credible survival plan. The most key example is the climate Armageddon which is actually unfolding in front of us, providing us with evidence of its existence on a daily basis. Yet the more sophisticated and accurate our climate data collection methods become, the more resistance builds against this evidence. This adverse reaction to the truth is a case for a great proportion of us, even for those who publicly claim to "believe" in climate change. Once you talk to them more privately, you begin to understand their inner denial voice: "But Earth has always changed" or "I just don't think its going to be all that bad really".

Apocalypse Does Not Compute

To better understand this denial it is important to consider again how our brain was originally wired, and the ultimate functions it was designed for. As mentioned earlier in this book, the human brain is a natural resource exploitation logistical device. As such, it needs to always remain creative and optimistic. But however imaginative, creative and innovative we can be as a species, we are tragically incompetent at catastrophizing: a much underrated skill which is looked down upon by our entire system, and for good reasons. Our brain was simply not made with the priority of considering and processing apocalyptic scenarios, unless we are blessed with Asperger's Syndrome or other neurodivergent ways of thinking which challenge the traditional survival-focused human brain.

As part of our brain's focus on creativity and innovation, it would seem that our default neural system has come with an in-built, yet malfunctioning Hope button. However dire things may be, the Hope button is permanently stuck in the On toggle position. But hope is the shortest, and surest path to delusion. Hope is like sugar: irresistible in the moment, but extremely corrosive in the long term. It is a friend when you're desperate for one, and at the same time a silent killer when you least suspect them. Yet we would much rather keep on aimlessly hoping, than actively work to create the conditions which would actually justify having a positive outlook in the first place.

A Brain Designed For A Different Era

Our obsession with stability and ignorance towards change, even as the latter takes place in front of our eyes, makes more sense once we consider the environment in which this particular brain evolved and developed its most hard-wired patterns of thinking. Our brain did not evolve in the midst of catastrophes, but during one of the most climatically stable and favourable times on the planet's geological history: there was an abundance of resources, and most importantly, a reliable, consistent and stable supply of these. There was real, actual stability and abundance back then, and our brain was designed for that era, not for today. This is why our brains will by design automatically assume that everything will be abundant, and most importantly, that it will stay that way. This also allows them to continue their creative, or destructive work, unhindered by any negative thoughts.

But that was then, and this is now. We live in a world which is hardly abundant anymore. 8 billion of us are fighting already over water and diminishing food resources, while more and more of the biome, which we depend upon, is driven to complete annihilation through extinction. Our brains developed at a time when there was never a need for "apocalypse brain". This is why today, despite all the stark and existential warnings, an apocalypse does not even make it to the top 10 list of humanity's preoccupations, and it is likely to be way below the latest news on Beyonce or Kim Kardashian, at any given point in time.

The Aspergers, the visionaries, the spiritual leaders, are the only ones throughout our history who had the ability to foresee disasters and envisage the right solutions. From Socrates to Nelson Mandela to Martin Luther King to Greta Thunberg, we have always labelled these people as Kassandras and "witches", hunted them down, and thrown them in jail because of "treason": they told us inconvenient truths which our brains were not made to comprehend, or contemplate. Instead, we preferred to perceive these inconvenient truths as personal threats, as they often challenged the very foundations of the social and economic systems which we had developed during this period of abundance.

We have evolved in a stability bubble. Any evidence which implies that "the world is ending" or "it is not what you thought it was" automatically sends our brains into "system cannot compute" mode. Denial is the way out of this impossible mental computation. Facing the reality is simply not part of our Human v1.0 brain software, or hardware for that matter.

Significant Cognitive Limitations

Of course, we are incredibly "smart" in other ways, most of them involving the immense data storage and processing capacity our brain is capable of. But this brain is a survival tool, first and foremost. It evolved specifically because humans with larger brains had better chances of devising ingenious survival solutions. Whether it was making things like tools, getting ourselves out of dangerous situations, or doing a Michael

Jackson moonwalk dance to attract a mate, the new brain gave us an incredible ability to link different pieces of information, and be able to imagine how they interact. We became self-aware in new ways: being able to think beyond our immediate vicinity, beyond the present, and beyond our current ecosystem.

But this was only rarely the existential type of thinking which philosophers practiced. In the majority of occasions, it was simply our in-built logistical device, modelling new and exciting scenarios for natural resource exploitation. It was this "scenario modelling", also called imagination, which increased our chances of survival. If only this ability to imagine and create was able to take things to the next level: imagining not only successes but also catastrophes, and actually taking action before they happen.

This cognitive limitation is accompanied by a type of arrogance and ignorance which is enough to dismiss facts and science which most people do not understand. The hostility which exists towards science experts is another sign of our primitive brain's denial and ignorance mechanisms acting up to "protect" us. Very few people have the basic training necessary to understand the quantitative concepts of scientific evidence, and override their brain's tendency to worship a false sense of stability. Perhaps the most famous scientific chart of all time, after Einstein's theory of relativity, is the one correlating carbon dioxide levels with the planet's temperature over the past hundreds of thousands of years. It very clearly and visually demonstrates the correlation between greenhouse gases and temperature, yet climate deniers will always invent the most ignorant, unsupported stories to refute the man-made origin of the climate crisis.

The Latent Cognition Of
The Tsunami Voyer

The chart demonstrates that we are at precisely the point where the raw egg has hit a hot pan: the egg is not cooked yet, but this is only because we are looking at a freeze-frame of the first split seconds. The egg looks perfectly translucent and raw on the hot pan. Until it actually starts changing color, we won't believe that it is cooked, because our "freeze frame" brain wants to believe in stability. Although in geological time scales this "freeze frame" represents a miniscule amount of time, it actually lasts for several decades in human years. This is the time it takes for the CO_2 to circulate through Earth's climate system and effect the temperature change that the graph predicts. We are currently living through the freeze-frame, which allows the climate sceptics to say "look, nothing is happening, it's all a hoax, probably need to turn up the stove a bit, as the egg isn't even cooking".

People struggle immensely with understanding this chart. Both the CO_2 y-axis scale and the x-axis timescale. They don't understand that there is a time lag between CO_2 and temperature. They don't understand confidence intervals, probabilities, extrapolation, and other mathematical and statistical concepts which tell us that there is a very ominous future already upon us.

Most of us still treat an official scientific prediction as "something that might happen", as opposed to a warning of what will actually happen. They are the same people you see in viral videos waiting to see a tsunami up close first, before they can believe it enough to start running. This is where the video usually cuts, skimming off the part where the "tsunami voyeur" drowns.

The climate crisis as a descriptive term will always be too abstract, general and scientific for the vast majority of people to connect with, or even understand - and even if they do, denial automatically will kick in as a protective mechanism. Climate-induced death, drought, flood, hunger and war however, are neither too abstract or too scientific. They are here, and we are experiencing them right now.

The 10-Minute Brain

But our powerful, charismatic brain has another major drawback: it is not made for long-term planning and projecting. Its impressive capacity to solve problems only functions if these problems are present right here, right now. From a survival point of view, the "right here right now" is much more important than 10 years from now, or even 10 minutes from now. There is no point in planning for the future if you cannot survive the next 10 minutes.

Long term planning therefore makes no sense whatsoever as a survival skill, from an evolutionary angle. Those who are best at surviving the next 10 minutes are much more likely to pass down their genes. For this reason, evolution concentrated on selecting brains that were really good at literally "surviving for today". One could argue therefore that the "right here right now" modality of our brain was further strengthened by evolution and became the dominant driver in our decision-making process.

If instead evolution had selected a brain which concentrated more on the long term consequences of our actions, we would all be a civilisation of dreamers and philosophers: dreamers may be intelligent, but they are too aloof and intellectual to pass on their genes, and much more likely to die while they are still mulling over the perfect solution. As a civilisation of dreamers, we would be great at imagining a sustainable future world, but we would be at risk of losing the plot on today, and literally not surviving the next 10 minutes. The in-depth rumination and analysis of the impacts of our decisions 10 years down the line would also possibly inhibit us from taking timely decisions in the present, and making those grandiose, audacious, risky plans which our civilisation is well known for, such as invading the country next door, or building the Tower of Babel. It is much better to take a sloppy decision in the next 10 minutes, than sit and think of the perfect decision, risking everything while the country next door decides to launch a surprise invasion instead. Our "fight or flight" responses are powerful, hormonal cascades which play out at the civilisation level, often overcoming any "stop and think" process.

It is easy to see how this would have played out in primitive times when we might have been faced with immediate and urgent dangers almost on a daily basis, therefore survival in "the next 10 minutes" being a real, palpable urgency. There was constant urgency and there were imminent life threats. There was never a "cosy day off" chilling at home watching Netflix, reading books, and writing apocalyptic dystopian fiction. We were too busy looking for the next meal or shelter. Evolution therefore selected a brain that could help us take care of the imminent problems in the present. If we didn't manage to survive today, there was no point in thinking about the future. All of the risks which our civilisation took along the way, some of which ended up paying off, would never have been taken if we had been making full projections and wasting time deliberating the perfect decision.

It is almost as if our brain had to develop a way to be naive and stupid to an extent, even as its processing power had dramatically increased. It had to remain as a "10-minute brain", even though it became smarter from a processing capacity perspective. This approach lowered the decision time to a survivable level. And it is potentially the reason why in-built mechanisms such as denial, delusion and the Hope button described earlier, are so strong in humans: they played a role in propelling our civilisation forward. They helped us narrow down our options and take those 10-minute decisions which were the most sloppy, selfish, yet effective options in the "right here, right now".

The downside was that we created a series of "10-minute civilisations", one after another, each one piling onto the next civilisation the unresolved long-term issues it had inherited from its predecessors. We are now living in the final civilisation, where these millenia-old issues cannot be ignored any longer.

Illusions of Intelligence

The 10-minute brain was a no-brainer (excuse the pun): in the era of abundance during which our civilisation and our brain evolved, almost all of our 10-minute risks would end up paying off. Our brain was tricked into thinking that it was actually intelligent, that it was taking the correct decisions, when in reality it was a spoiled brain which got lucky in an era of abundance: it became used to getting away with one mistake after another. The dominant model of civilisation became: 1) exploit the local area to death 2) pack up and leave for a fresh area. More than 80 civilisations learned this wrong lesson: that it is OK to ruin natural resources, because once everything is destroyed, you just pack up and move somewhere else. Obviously, today this is not an option. But our 10-minute brain is all we have.

Today, thanks to our education, technology and data tools, we are finally able to project well into the future. But whatever our data may show us, the evidence still has to go through the final filter of our primitive 10-minute brain, before any decision can be taken. The long-term impacts of the climate crisis have been known for many decades, yet our decision-making capacity remains subject to denial, delusion, the Hope button, and so on.

Obviously our primitive brain is winning the cognitive battle. Never before did we have so many data tools and technologies to measure, monitor and predict our own collapse, yet somehow be completely incapacitated in taking the myriad of difficult yet very straightforward decisions we need to take, and the corresponding policies we need to implement - all of which have been clear to us for a very long time. The climate crisis is not registered as a "next 10 minutes" crisis in our brain, even though it is entirely existential.

We Are Obsolete Hardware

The trouble of course with evolution is that it can only respond to current circumstances, not future ones. It will select for the genes and gene mutations which suit the current environment: the current predators, dangers, and climatic and living conditions. In fact, evolution is always playing a catch-up game with time, and it is terribly inefficient at that. As a species we are only as good as our previous "working" version. Selecting and eliminating mutations, the process of evolution, takes many, many generations. Our planet is currently changing so fast that evolution can barely keep up with it. Most extinction events happened because climatic conditions changed too rapidly for species to develop evolutionary adaptations.

In addition to a rapidly changing climate, humans today are faced with multiple existential crises, all of which are culminating simultaneously: overpopulation, water shortage, ecological destruction and annihilation of the food web, artificial intelligence to mention just a few. Even if these crises crossed-over into the "10 minute survival interval" so that our primitive brain can register them, it would be too late to address them, given their magnitude, complexity and interconnectedness. These are crises stemming from decisions we took thousands of years ago. Most of the solutions should have been taken hundreds of years ago, and many could have been taken just in the past few decades.

Instead, we have reached today's point of no return. Multiple tipping points have been crossed already, a major one being Earth's inability to absorb our emissions. The planet is well on its way to becoming a wasteland. More heat means more dissapearing forests and ocean marine life, which means more carbon in the atmosphere, which means more heat. We have now entered an irreversible acceleration path, literally rolling down the hill faster and faster until there is nothing left to burn, even if we tried to halt this process.

Our 10-minute survival strategies are obviously obsolete. They have not done us any favours, as we are now facing the long-term consequences of those bad decisions taken a very long time ago, when our civilisation was forming its habits and norms. Fossil fuel as an energy source was great back in the day, not today. Almost all of our technologies, innovations and other survival strategies have followed the 10-minute survival modality: they tend to have immense short term benefits, but punishing long-term consequences: resource depletion, consumerism, elimination of other species and habitats, all have had tremendously positive effects for humanity in the short term. But we are now living the era of consequences. This is a war between two brains: The brain that only cares about right now, and the brain which we have not fully developed, which is able to project into next year. It is very clear who is winning.

We may think we are intelligent, and we are indeed numerically intelligent when it comes to seeing patterns in data, putting together models, and identifying solutions. But overriding all of this is the primitive survival brain focused only on today. It is the same brain which led Nobel Prize economists across the world to conclude that there is no Financial Crisis on the way, and that all those sub prime residential mortgages will somehow pay themselves off. Even the climate scientist who knows what is coming will surrender to reality and go home every night to their kids, earn their salary, and focus on getting to survive the next week, or at least, the next 10 minutes.

We may be creating next generation iphones, but when it comes to our brain we are still using "Humans v1.0" when we should be on v5.0 by now. The climate crisis will not be solved using old hardware, and human brains right now are as obsolete as Kodak photographic film: out of place, out of time, and off topic. There may be 8 billion of us on this planet, but as a species we might as well already be considered functionally extinct. Our civilisation is eating itself, the food chain cannot support us anymore, and Earth has turned against us with every possible weapon it could muster. All this because the very hardware of our brains, what makes us who we are, has become obsolete in this new world: ironically, a world of our own making.

The Great Procrastination

The irresistible urge to focus on "right here right now" has been further strengthened by a capitalist economy which encourages impulse buying, instant gratification and single-use / short-lifetime products,. This is increasingly pronounced in many of our modern psychological coping mechanisms and addictions: we seek short term satisfaction in unhealthy foods, drugs, and other habits because they make us feel good right here, right now. But the duration of response is getting shorter and shorter. Everything now in our civilisation is about the next 10 minutes. Issues which are more long-term and cannot be addressed right now, issues which require patience and thinking, are put off forever. In fact, they are completely aborted.

This is happening at a time when everything on this planet is being rearranged, reconfigured, rerouted, rewired, reassembled, from scratch. The planet is moving its weather systems around like it was furniture, leaving us to wonder: "This wall wasn't here. The TV is upside down. Why is there a hole in the roof? This isn't even my neighbourhood". Everything is undergoing rapid change as the climate catastrophe takes hold, yet this change is still not within the 10-minute mark. What will certainly not change is the primitive brain of the species which brought all of this chaos about. This old brain won't survive this.

At a time when our civilisation should be switching to a long-term thinking mindset, we are literally heading the opposite direction. For a civilisation that has developed so many complex, advanced scientific disciplines, it is astounding that the very simple math of the human overpopulation bomb, by far the biggest factor in the climate crisis , has been silenced and censored by this necrocapitalist system. The survival of these 8 billion humans continues to depend upon the destruction of everything that moves, lives and breathes on this planet. This is a survival model which will undoubtedly soon become unsurvivable.

Somewhere in this galaxy, it is possible that there is a solar system with an intelligent species who may have just about managed to avoid destroying itself. Based on what we know about Earth so far, the chances are that civilisations elsewhere also follow the 10-minute model. Like flickering stars, they would be lucky if they ever overlapped.

PLANET OF THE NARCISSISTS

A World of Worlds

For a small planet, Earth harbors an incredible diversity of terrains and microclimates, even if the biosphere were to be excluded. It is nothing short of a miracle how a single celestial object can be host to so many landscapes, life forms and ecosystems. We live in a "world of worlds", all of which coexist within this barely noticeable, lonely rock revolving around itself in an otherwise dark, cold, silent infinity of emptiness. The level of wealth on Earth, compared to the black desert which surrounds it, becomes even more apparent at the molecular level: while there may only be 8 million species on this planet, the molecular diversity of carbon compounds they represent approaches infinity. This is the magnitude of what is at stake on Earth. As more of the biome goes extinct, we are losing it forever before we can even appreciate how incredibly diverse it is. Every single life form on this planet, no matter how small, contains within it a unique molecular and genetic treasure trove that has taken billions of years to evolve. All the money in the world, all the minerals, oil, property or other measure of wealth, are collectively not even worth one, single life form going extinct.

To pay respect to the natural world is to recognize each and every species' invaluable, irreproducible uniqueness, as well as the incredibly long evolutionary journey it has made over billions of years to become adapted to this planet. As we make Earth uninhabitable, we are throwing all this away, reducing the planet back down to its basic elements. All we are is matter which travels from one being to the next, from inanimate minerals to organic lifeforms, and back. But rather than celebrating the diverse chemical links which connect us, by birth and death, to other beings, we keep on poisoning the very circle which ultimately links back to us. And we put 150 life forms out of existence daily.

Surreal Clockwork

Our story, the story of Earth, couldn't possibly be more surreal and miraculous at the same time. Even the smartest team of human designers would almost certainly have failed to imagine, not least create, our world from scratch - even if they had access to all the tools and elements in the periodic table. How could they succeed, after all, since they themselves are a mere tiny piece of this creation? They would miss the mark by a long shot.

The planet's "designers" would probably think that trees are thermodynamically impossible: how can these huge complex structures support their weight in the wind, towering over the land, sometimes hundreds of feet tall? How could they "grow and expand from the inside", and produce millions of bright green leaves that feed on just thin air (CO_2) and water? How would they cope in winter? The very thought of a tree sounds impossible, too good to be true. It sounds like someone's acid trip. Yet this miracle of life exists.

The same designers would not even know where to start when assembling the planet's climate machine, and its renewable, cyclical processes: a collection of interdependent systems which recirculate temperature, water, nutrients, magma, air, electrical charge, radiation and oxygen throughout the planet in ways that are too ingenious for us to fully understand. This is a living planet where everything is recycled, including civilizations.

Yet all these seemingly chaotic processes are in balance with each other. All these terrains and microclimates, all these very different worlds, these dynamic and often aggressive and antagonizing processes, are in full communication with each other via the Earthnet of Things. The level of complexity of the Earth's machine is so vast, so deep, that it will never be fully understood by humans, and possibly even a deep mind AI. Earth is a Swiss watch with an infinite number of gears, springs and feedback loops, and even living beings are an active part of its central mechanism.

Orbiting Towards Unconsciousness

The Swiss watch is normally able to self-tune. But humans are the one "rogue gear" in this watch, who does not want to be regulated by the other gears. It wants to spin on its own, however it likes to, whenever it likes to. Humans still know very little about the climate of this planet, because they are treating it as a collection of independent gears. They still fail to see that all the gears need to work together, they are connected, meaning that everything you do on Earth will eventually come back to you.

The planet's climate is therefore a mere reflection of ourselves, a reaction to the actions we are putting into the Swiss watch. Depending on our behaviour, we get the climate we deserve. We have chosen to disregard the rules of the Swiss watch, and bring it all down. The climate Armagedon we are experiencing is therefore a direct mirror into who we are as a society. As our civilisation overheats from its own by-products, wars and psychoses, so does the planet. The climate is directly mirroring the chaos of our unsustainable, self-destructive and dysfunctional civilization. We, are the rogue gear in the watch. And our actions have already damaged the watch beyond repair.

Missing The Watch For The Gears

Despite all our efforts and scientific endeavors, it is becoming clear that we are too small to understand the big picture of this planet - and to see the forest, not the trees: to be able to see the Swiss watch as one, whole being that needs every single one of its gears in working order, so that it can operate. The forest may be burning, but as we become consumed by our narcissism, all that we see is mirages of ourselves in the flames. We lack both the consciousness and the humility to recognize our predicament, and both of these are fundamental cognitive handicaps.

Our arrogance has been central to this: humans have made the tragic error of mistaking their narcissism for self-awareness. While self-awareness imparts infinite vision, vanity is a lethal form of myopia, at best. Without true awareness, there is no true intelligence. This civilisation prides itself in being self-aware, yet bizarrely it has never cared about its survival in the longer term. This is because it has fundamentally been in denial about where it comes from, and has absolutely no idea where it is going.

Arrogance, naivety and narcissism have been repeat offenders throughout our history. As we made modifications and upgrades to the Swiss watch, we have always been blind to the downsides which these modifications may bring. We casually accepted the negative impacts of our technological achievements, tolerating them as minor side effects which would surely be balanced out at some point, by both short and long-term benefits. They never were. History proved us wrong on multiple occasions, and now we have reached the point where the watch has been tampered with too many times. It is a Frankenstein watch made up of the wrong parts, and about to have a heart attack any minute now.

We naively disturbed this planet's ecosystems and weather systems for our own benefit, not realising that if the rest of the gears in this watch cannot work properly, eventually the entire system malfunctions. As we continue to be the rogue gear in this watch, we face an existential Armageddon. Our destruction of the planet's climate is the ultimate result of a blind, parasitic civilisation which falsely assumed it had the luxury of taking unilateral decisions. We may think we are safely observing from the control room as the yet another bomb we have invented detonates. But this bomb is the big one, and possibly the final one. It will take out everything, including the control room. The time on the watch, is now only seconds away from midnight.

Loss of Consciousness

How did we turn out to be so terminally blind? It would seem that our cognitive function has followed a direction opposite to that of our technological progress. There are a number of ways in which this paradox is unfolding:

First, we have been nurturing an economic system whose very survival depends on keeping us unhappy and hungry for products. The more unhappy, unsatisfied and greedy we become, the more we turn inwardly and lose sight of this world. Not only do we become too narcissistic to appreciate and value this planet, but we also literally become blind: we cannot see it. Present, past, future, all merge into one, as we lose sense of time and space and become obsessed with our personal image and our "stuff". This has become the planet of the narcissists. Necrocapitalism is taking us on a journey towards full unconsciousness, with tragic consequences.

The first casualty of unconsciousness is the loss of a moral compass. We have created a society where if something is not sellable, or doesn't get any monetizable "air time", then it is absolutely useless. Values such as dignity, compassion, equality, healthcare, environmentalism, are often red alerts for our system: they are loss-makers, extremely risky areas for our capitalist society to "invest" in. They only become profitable when hijacked and weaponized as temporary facades for political campaigns, green new deals or clever product marketing, so that they can appeal to whatever humanity is left in us before we enter the voting booth. Governments, brands, sometimes even charities, have learned to play the "equality" card very well whenever they need the votes, pretending to support minorities and LGBTQ rights. The more "woke" our culture becomes, the more it seems that there has never been a time when humans have been so out of touch with their own humanity.

Gone Missing: Gratitude, Empathy

Unconsciousness also means being unable to appreciate just about anything and everything. Most modern humans are blind to the natural miracle which surrounds them on this planet in every waking moment of their existence. In our futile search to constantly implement the most shallow, meaningless improvements to our lifestyles, we easily forget what is already here, free of charge: a planet where the sun will rise every morning, the grass will be green, the ecosystem and the climate system will be there to continue to nurture us.

We had it all, already. But by taking all this creation for granted, we forgot long ago that it too, needs attention and maintenance. To truly appreciate this planet is to realize that all these "pretty" life forms we like to watch in our documentaries are extremely fragile living organisms, just like us: they need light, water, oxygen, nutrients, love and protection during every minute of their existence. Extinction is the greatest disrespect towards the legacy of this planet's creation. It is an irreversible curse that will follow us forever. These are species who we will never know, and who will never know us.

Following the strategy of a typical narcissist, humanity has always focused on the immediate next step, never thinking for a minute of the long term repercussions on the people and beings it had to manipulate in order to achieve its goals.   Things do not always necessarily improve. They can also deteriorate, very rapidly.

We Are All Products Now

Yet another avenue through which we have become unconscious is by being converted into products within the new digital psychonomy. Necrocapitalism is pushing every life form and every renewable resource towards its death sentence: the supermarketization route, and humans themselves are not excluded from this.

The role of the consumer is no longer limited to buying products.   They themselves are up for sale, an ingenious innovation of necrocapitalism which has allowed the generation of new sources of revenue.   The way it works is that each of us is now a monetizable and tradeable data set, therefore an information asset which can be sold off to the very corporations we were already giving money to as consumers. So it is like we are paying twice: once for the products we buy, then for helping corporations make more money from us by surrendering our data to them, completely for free. Google and Facebook have re-invented consumatrons as precious datasets, whose data can be bought, sold, influenced and exploited, and they are making billions by selling us all off to whoever, whenever, wherever they like.

But there is yet another twist, yet another role which the consumer has assumed, on behalf of the psychonomic farm: they have become unsuspecting, but fully willing, workers within the digital supermarket. All of us are being increasingly enlisted to do the dirty work of the tech companies and corporations, by treating other humans as products as well. Our interactions on social media may appear to be interactions with other humans, but they are in fact yet another way to monetize us: whether we are scrolling through Instagram, Facebook, Tinder or TikTok, all we are doing is feeding the algorithms which the Thing operates on, simply by choosing where we allocate our "Likes". Each Like is yet another datapoint for the Thing.

In other words, the consumer today is more than just a consumer. They are a digital slave with three distinct roles, all of which serve the digital psychonomy. The first role is to buy products. The second role is to exist as a free, monetizable dataset. And the third is to actually work for the psychonomy for free, expanding the algorithms of its vast dataset with each social media interaction they make, or purchasing touchpoint they use.

There is of course very little human consciousness in this process, as it is all increasingly driven and monetized by algorithms. Our digital dystopia is incredibly sophisticated and developed, and already has far more of a grip on us at this stage than we would ever have imagined.

Supermarketization of
Human Relationships

The repercussions of supermarketization on our ethics are catastrophic. Our digital psychonomy is habituating us into treating other humans as products or web pages that we scroll through. We increasingly interact both with humans and other life forms on a purely transactional basis: viewing them as items on our "want" list, as opposed to independent entities with their own rights, wants and feelings. Whether it is an employee we are about to hire, a friend that we turn to only at a time of need, or a potential partner that we swipe left or right on Tinder, the "browsing" process is beginning to resemble that of hastily going through a clothes rack in a vintage shop: we never stop to think, to consider the rich legacy and history each item carries with it, and which is not reflected in the value on the price tag. In this distraction and consumption psychonomy, we never seem to afford other life forms, whether human or not, the attention which they deserve, and which goes way beyond simply being objects for acquisition.

Our police forces increasingly see people as objects, treating protesters as obstacles in a video game. Soon it will become easier to program compassion into a robot, rather than "re-program" compassion into our human police force. The Robocop age will soon become reality, as we rely on algorithms to maintain social cohesion. Yearly surveys conducted by city authorities in the future will reassure citizens: "new survey finds that robot police forces continue to be more effective, more compassionate, and less racist than real humans".

The incredible irony is that the more hyper-narcissistic we become within this digital dystopia, the more of ourselves we are giving away completely for free, to the algorithmocracy which operates this system. We have been conned, yet again, in the most spectacular way.

People in the wealthier areas of the world are the most unconscious of us all. As capitalism automates more and more of our lives with amenities and luxuries that we take for granted, we become even more blind and ungrateful. Like a tenant who has just moved into a new flat, there are certain things like air, food, water, the right temperature, which they falsely assume are included as standard in the contract. We take for granted the very resources which we destroy. We falsely think that all these amenities "came with the planet", as if they were a minutes and data package from a phone company. We've had the package and the rented flat for so many millions of years now, and we've forgotten that in order to maintain it and not be evicted from the flat, we have to also stick to our end of the bargain: don't trash the place.

Death by Entertainment

Entertainment has become a major driver for the psychonomy, being a daily staple for an increasingly narcissistic consumatron base. Entertainment has managed to merge with everything: whereas before it was confined to activities and events clearly identified as light amusement, it is now used as a powerful tranquilizer to deflect and normalise serious social issues which are not, and should not be entertaining to any of us. Almost anything and everything can now end up in a morning TV show, where it is downplayed and given "the popcorn treatment" so that viewers feel that the world is still in place, and that they can all go to their necrocapitalist jobs in good spirits.

People love to be entertained. They love it even more when serious issues are presented to them as a funny story which they can simply laugh at, then put it aside but still feel that they have "addressed it". In these dystopian TV shows, serious news are bizarrely mixed in with celebrity gossip in order to downgrade, disarm and effectively censor any inconvenient truth. The nitrous media have even managed to turn the climate crisis and the end of civilisation into a benign morning coffee break. Whereas our instinctive reaction to floods, fires and other concerning news is to be alarmed, concerned, or even panic, the way in which these news are presented to us manages to calm us down, and make us numb to reality. News of heatwaves are served to us with images of people eating ice cream at the beach. Floods are presented as rain or light disruption. And forest fires pay more attention to the temporary air quality issues, rather than the destruction of yet another carbon sink which will push us further into the climate and ecological apocalypse.

Hollywoodization of Nature

Our natural world has similarly been turned into a theme park, rather than the collapsing ecosphere that it is. We do marvel at the most exotic aspects of our planet, often sitting mesmerised for hours in front of our TVs watching David Attenborough documentaries. But this takes on more of an hedonistic entertainment value, as we become voyers looking for instant gratification. We don't really care about these life forms. Like visiting a theme park, you pay your ticket and get your day's worth of fun, as your eyes move from one display to another, one fun ride to the next, without ever contemplating the significance of the things that you are seeing or experiencing.

Whether they are fish, trees or colorful birds, we have stopped seeing them as life forms and have begun to treat them as entertainment objects, or at best, as actors playing in their own, sad, autobiographical movie. We have confused real life, and the real significance of the creation, with meaningless entertainment. Every life form becomes an object which looks just like the original, but without a soul, and without any rights of its own. It has been supermarketized, objectified for our entertainment, and tucked away in a dusty supermarket shelf. In our ignorant eyes, it has effectively become lifeless.

Once the nature documentary finishes and the popcorn runs out, our attention needs to switch to the next excitement which our capitalist theme park has in store for us, from an endless database of personalized auto-suggestions. Everything that we've just seen, all the actors and actresses of the plant and animal kingdom, only existed for our entertainment, not for themselves. They were not part of our reality. Any meaningful attachment to them or appreciation of their existence vanishes immediately, as the next program begins.

Own or Die

It is no wonder then that our instinctive reaction to any stimulus, life form or object, is whether we can own it or not. We have become the consumatrons our psychonomy wanted us to be. The natural resource logistical exploitation device is becoming more and more focused. But what is at stake, what is in fact being eroded, is our very humanity. Our psychonomy has made greed the central inner compass which directs all of our interactions, and it has made ownership, the urge to buy, our go-to instinct in how we interact with everything - something profoundly ironic given that all of us are practically owned by this system. We are much more interested in owning things than learning about them, empathizing with them, understanding them and simply respecting their right to exist, as themselves, in their natural setting. However many documentaries we make, morning TV shows we host or museums we build, they will never capture the soul and the essence of these life forms, because in our eyes they have become lifeless digital actors and actresses. Our obsession with "cataloguing" the natural world, although seemingly harmless, is an example of this mental disorder of obsessive ownership. We count species in numbers, like bottles of detergent sitting on a supermarket shelf, completely forgetting that these are fragile beings.

There are no limits to the benevolence we could be demonstrating towards both ourselves and the planet, if only we realised that we own nothing. Everything in our possession is borrowed from the real owner, Earth: even the molecules of our body, the vessel of our ego.

IN THE GRIP OF NECROCAPITALISM

It Is Alive And Intelligent

Evolution has come a long way - perhaps longer than we thought, or at least had been taught in school. We would like to believe that we, humans, represent the forefront of evolution on Earth. But arguably there are other forms of existence here on this planet which supersede us, including some which precede us. One of the most recent of these is our own economic system: a logistical intelligence network which may have been originally developed by humans to serve humans, but is now coming to the ponit where it can think for itself, and serve only itself. Although humans are its original creators, they have been demoted and reduced to a mere resource within the wider system: they are there as maintenance workers who continue to engineer its expansion, while at the same time being exploited and monetized by it. Then, they are simply thrown away. It is a bizarre symbiosis which has taken millennia to evolve, like many bizarre symbioses found in Earth's ecosystem. What keeps humans enslaved to this system, is the de facto foundation that profit should be the goal of any advanced social organisation. The hard financial figures of business now rule everything on this planet. Everything else is secondary, including humans themselves.

At the most fundamental level, a life form is defined as an entity which can replicate itself. Our psychonomic system is so efficient, so adaptable and vicious in its search for profit, that it partially fulfills the criteria to be classified not only as a life form all to itself, but also as a semi-sentient one. Nothing can kill it, not even its creators, who have become both servants and dependents within it. This system has proven to be the ultimate predatory life form: able to survive on scraps here and there, and even eat itself if it needs to. Most of all, it can feed on death itself. It thrives on expiration dates, diminishing resources, extinction, fast fashion, multiple forms of slavery and planned obsolescence. It owes its existence and persistence to its ability to live out of the carcass of its own mother, the Earth, even as the latter becomes poorer and poorer. It is a death cult, and it is time to start refering to it by its real name: necrocapitalism.

If all of this sounds too much like the Matrix movie series, think about why we are heading full speed towards self-destruction. The reason why we have not solved the climate crisis and overshoot of our civilisation yet is because we are not the ones in control of our destiny. Our psychonomic system is in control of everything now: it is our boss, keeping us in check with alarm clocks, salaries and consumer propaganda. We live under the delusion that we have developed an economic system which works for us, when in reality we are the ones working, being exploited. What we have in fact created is our own slave master: one who is always ready to discard us, if we dare not participate. Whether this system represents a higher or lower form of intelligence than us, it really doesn't matter. What matters is who has the upper hand, and it's not us anymore.

In order to avoid a pointless, philosophical and narcissistically human-centric debate on the sentience or not of this system, I will resort for now to refer to this necrocapitalist entity as the "Thing", also to avoid direct comparisons with DNA-based biological life forms. Some people, including myself, may at times refer to the Thing as capitalism. Others may refer to it as a form of artificial intelligence.

Alas, The First Suicidal Life Form on Earth

Whatever we decide to call this system, the big problem with the Thing is that it is by definition self-destructive. It is a resource-syphoning system driven by profit and efficiency alone, aimed at maximum utilization of resources to the point of exhaustion.

In other words, it follows maximum death / maximum profit economics. This monstrous progeny of our greed, The Thing, now runs this planet. It operates not on dreams, laughter, tears, feelings, aspirations, creativity, spontaneity, love, compassion or any other of our best human qualities. It operates on profit until death. It is a system of necrocapitalism which is self-programmed to implode, once it has used up all of its raw materials.

The whole point of business is to utilize (deplete) all of its raw materials as fast as possible. This is today's definition of business success. Once you realise this, it becomes abundantly clear why Earth, and us, are already finished. This process is increasingly taking an algorithmic character, moving further and further out of the direct control of humans, who are merely assisting engineers of the Thing. Regardless of how one describes it or names it, the economic system humans have created has taken over and now has a mind of its own. It owns us, the Earth and all of its resources, and it will deplete everything before it turns the gun to its head. The Thing has been programmed by humans to be a beast that never sleeps. It never knows how to pace itself or conserve its energy. Its remit is to keep going, until one day suddenly, it can't - and it collapses. Even those who still nurture high hopes on solving the climate emergency and are exploring solutions to taking control of the Thing so that e.g. we can manage our carbon emissions, admit more or less that the only realistically feasible way to reform this system would need to be so drastic that it would literally feel like we are starting all over.

This is actually not far from the truth. Our entire civilisation has been built on the premise of expansion until self-destruction. This means that the very foundations of the society we have been building for thousands of years now, would need to change. Is that even possible? Given that we have operated a self-destructive psychonomic model for

200 thousand years, suddenly moving to a non-necrocapitalist system with sustainability and regeneration at its heart would not be a "shift" or a "reform". It would need to be a revolution of civilisational proportions. The only way to reform the Thing is to kill it. This is very difficult, given that the Thing itself is suicidal. It is not afraid of death. It will bet its own life in the climate casino. It will take any and every risk to come back.

Dumb Against Dumber

Killing the Thing of course implies the collapse of many, but maybe not all, of the edifices of our civilization which have an existential dependency on it. But very few admit this dark truth publicly. This is why, for every pragmatic and honest book on this subject matter, there are twenty more utopian, "hopeful" ones advocating unrealistic solutions which could only have been implemented in another universe, by a much more intelligent being: one that does not simply have intelligence, but wisdom as well. Whatever intelligence humans may have had, it has overwhelmingly been sidelined long ago by the greed-related psychoses that our necrocapitalist system has been selecting for, again and again over millenia of social evolution. Even if we were to kill the Thing, we would be left with the same human brain: one that is highly susceptible to economic approaches which use maximum destruction, and therefore self-destruction, as their main resource utilisation model.

A Human Imposter

But aside from the climate crisis, which is on track to end human civilization and much of life on Earth, there is another reason why it is paramount to at least try and eliminate the Thing. We all need to realize that we are not it, and it is not us. The Thing doesn't care about humans, in much the same way that it doesn't care about its own eventual self-destruction. It is a threat to humanity and has no respect for its original creators. Although the Thing is enmeshed in our society, and we think we control it and live within it and around it, it in fact controls us. It mirrors some of our tendencies and may appear to be human, but it is not really part of us. It has no concern for, or preoccupation with, the multi-faceted interests and existential needs of humans, and only focuses on the hard, cold figures of its business bottom line. Any economic system which sees nature and human rights as threats to its bottom line is self-destructive and doomed to consume itself.

Humanity has convinced itself that the Thing is the best economic system: offering the fastest, biggest returns, at a cost that can be deferred to unborn, future generations. Consumption, overpopulation, growth, are the toxic outcomes of this economic dogma. The more this civilisation refuses to acknowledge the unsustainable foundations of its existence, the more it confirms that its ultimate destiny is to self-annihilate.

It is important to understand the power that the Thing now has over us, and by no means am I trying to transfer the massive responsibility humans have for the state of the planet to an abstract nebulous entity. We created the Thing, exactly because it embodied and executed our vision of domination and greed, but we have come to the point where the Thing has completely hijacked the central nervous system of human civilisation. More accurately, it has co-evolved with us as an internal parasite.

The Ultimate Exploitation Machine

The Thing is a device, an optimized machine which is an extension of the human brain, another logistical device. Humans, if anything, are rarely truly intelligent, nor are they fully self-aware. They are simply very efficient in resource appropriation and exploitation. This is not intelligence by any measure, but a type of skill. The Thing is a steroid-infused extension of our skillset, with orders of magnitude more processing power than us, which unintentionally got out of control and now unfortunately has the upper hand.

The problem with "skills" such as these is that they eventually become outdated. True intelligence, which both us and the Thing lack, has a much longer lifetime. Without true intelligence, we are stuck with developing tools which end up taking a life of their own, taking over us, and turning us into mere peripheral, expendable components within a semi-sentient self-destructive ecosystem of skills.

This is an evolution lesson that may be too dark, dystopian, and difficult to swallow to ever be taught in schools. But there is a strong case to be made that our destiny, by all accounts and historical measures so far, is to eventually self-annihilate by becoming part of a biomechanical symbiosis that eventually either engulfs us, or gets rid of us altogether at the next software update.

The Only Ponzi Game In Town

It takes considerable effort to begin to see the Thing, given that all of us are so incredibly enmeshed within it in every possible way. Like a true symbiont, it provides us with protection in exchange for taking over our lives and the planet, and this is why many of us will defend the Thing to our death. Like coral and algae on a reef, consumers and the Thing are seemingly forever locked into a symbiotic relationship: in effect we are the algae, doing all the photosynthetic work which produces food for the coral, which is the Thing. All that the Thing/coral does is provide us with protection, just like a Mafia boss or a pimp who handles our salary and our food and board arrangements. This Ponzi scheme economic system traumatizes us every single day, offering us digital entertainment and social app "likes" as a deflective "apology". These are are in fact merely temporary painkillers, aiming to prevent us from opting out of the reef altogether.

We have long ago stopped existing as free-form algae. By the age of 15, most of us have already become greedy consumers living in a colorful theme park made of corruption, exploitation and extinction. Our transformation from aspiring thinking beings to consumer zombies is almost complete. The algae has stopped thinking of itself as independent. It has become part of its own dystopian symbiosis, its co-dependent relationship with its pimp.

The "reef" is unfortunately only visible from a far enough distance which allows a panoramic view of the Thing, and its complete grip on us. Only those with special eyes and ears can see and hear the nightmare that we have created. Only those who have briefly rejected the mass-manufactured luxuries, lullabies and narcotics of the psychonomy can begin to see the Thing for what it really is: a planet-eating machine.

Enter The Puppets

The Thing of course is also completely in charge of all power structures and the government. The problem with authority will always be that it cares more about maintaining itself than about serving the well-being of the people it was meant to represent. This is true regardless of who is in power. Therefore, the role of all governments is, and has always been, to maintain the self-destructive economic system which brought the government to power in the first place. This ensures that there is no change of government, which is the first and foremost goal of every political party. In this sense, it can be argued that both government and religion are servants of the Thing: they came into existence to protect economic oligarchs, by manipulating people into submission. Economic oligarchs in turn are the direct engineers of the Thing.

In fact, the only type of economy which humans have experienced in the last few hundred years is one where the Thing increasingly dominates everything. Over millennia we matured into an elaborate web of laws, religions, governance systems and technologies enabling wealth accumulation through the widespread theft of people, beings, and the resources they were originally meant to share. We refer to this as civilization, but it is only one possible version of it. Our profit-obsessed society has become nothing but a 24-hour sweatshop which only serves profit. In this pointless rat race, no one is allowed to stand still, to stay content, or stay in the present. We are all working zombies. We are all working for the Thing

The Numerization of Everything

The industrial revolution was the point when this civilisation completely lost it. Like a virus, it became more concerned with making infinite copies of itself, rather than contemplating the meaning and purpose of that which it was making copies of. This was also the time when our society officially shifted from qualitative to quantitative measures of success. A narrative of continued economic growth and procreation, the very toxic time bomb which will end both the Thing and us, had to be developed by both governments and religion in order to continue propping up the psychonomy. Today, all leaders have espoused this narrative, and they feel obliged to talk about achieving an economic and population boost for their nations, many of them knowing very well that the pursuit of such growth ultimately guarantees a spectacular extinction for almost every life form on Earth, including themselves.

But they cannot change their propaganda. The political survival of these leaders, not to mention the credit rating of entire nations they represent, is dependent on the necrocapitalist metrics the Thing uses to measure and monitor the psychonomy. Even people themselves are not seen as humans anymore, but as singular GDP units. Our metrics-driven world has forever redefined happiness: there is an obsession to measure it, in ever so many different quantitative ways, rather than to simply experience it, and allow people to evaluate it and pursue it based on their own personal criteria. This fundamentally limits their prospects of ever attaining it.

Money Corrupts Value

Money Corrupts People

This numerization of happiness started long ago, once value was expressed as money and became abstract currency - making the real, tangible meaning and value of things invisible to humans. Because money emphasized quantity of supply and demand, and not actual quality of life or value of goods, it would soon become an object of mindless and abstract accumulation, where the accumulation goal had no stop point. If the object of accumulation is apples, we stop at the point where we feel we have enough apples to feed our family. However when the objective is to accumulate money, there is no upper ceiling. We can keep going, forever.

This concept of abstract accumulation naturally further supported the growth paradigm of expansion and leveraging. It can in fact be argued that the death sentence to the planet was set the minute money was invented. Money became the vehicle behind the acceleration of this self-destructive psychonomy, as it supercharged greed and universalised it into just one, simple "object" to acquire: coins or paper notes. The fact that everyone had these, also made comparisons between people much more visible, given that all people were now easily compared against each other, and against the same type of coin or paper note. This undoubtedly increased competition, and therefore greed.

The Birth Of Necrocapitalism

The other problem with abstract currencies, such as the human monetary system, is that they assign value in unfair, often arbitrary ways, mostly based on supply. Because of this uncoupling between monetary value and real, tangible value, everything and everyone is at risk of becoming undervalued, devalued, and eventually extinct. In fact, the destruction of renewable resources and the invention of single use products like throwaway fashion, have been essential prerequisite elements of the Thing. Products which die or break down have much more value to the Thing, as they ensure more products will be made to replace the "broken" ones. This engineered and premature death is the main operating model behind necrocapitalism.

Necrocapitalism operates a lethal business plan whereby in order to monetize Earth, the planet itself in its entirety has to become a single-use commodity. Much like with smartphones, computers and other devices that are purposely made to break down after a few months or years, we have made Earth obsolescent. We've condemned an entire planet to death, just to make a few dollars which will soon mean nothing.

But planets are not single-use commodities. A new planet will not, and cannot be made, once it is broken. This planet, the only planet we have, is being converted to trash and entered, in its entirety, into the necrocapitalist conveyor belt of single-use death. There are hardly any products in our civilization, for the birth of which something or someone didn't have to die, be exploited, or even go extinct. In fact, almost everything man-made is cursed with the karma of a spurned planet.

The Human (necro) Capital

This erosion of value of course extends to humans themselves, and is witnessed in the devaluing of the average employee who would like to be seen as a human being, but becomes a disposable pair of hands instead. All of the crimes which humanity has perpetrated on this planet, it has also perpetrated on itself: destruction, extinction, exploitation are not simply unfortunate side effects of our civilisation, but essential elements in the operating fabric of the functioning psychonomy. We live in a world where real, value-producing jobs have become cheap resources to be exploited by those who have the so-called "bullshit jobs", which simply push paper and shift blame and responsibility. At the top of this food chain sit those who are wealthy enough to the point where their only job is to spend, consume, and ensure that those they exploit remain vulnerable - and therefore fully exploitable. Most of us are embedded in busy careers with companies that damage people, places and the environment just so that they can turn a profit and pay our salaries. The psychonomy is destroying both the employee and the planet, converting them to single-use commodities.

Billions of people go to work each day, have their Teams chats, coffees, sandwiches, and then go shopping, enslaved to an economic system which is killing this planet. But this is all temporary. When the sandwiches run out, it will already be too late. And there will be no point to any meetings, jobs, movies, and all other consumatronic distractions. As long as the Thing is in charge, this is the ultimate outlook for the planet.

The Trio of Fools

There is a tripartite toxic feedback loop between leaders, voters and economic oligarchs which is not really of any significance, given that they are all puppets of each other, entangled in co-dependent relationships. Voters are either too brainwashed or powerless to effect any change, while leaders cannot turn their backs on the economic oligarchs who brought them to power, and who provide the jobs to voters. Therefore, unless all three groups wake up at the same time, we are looking at the worst case scenario for the future of the planet. The elephant in the room who is actually, really in charge of this entire puppet show is the Thing. A humanity that restores the planet will never take root using today's social, political and economic systems, as long as these systems are completely under the control and influence of the Thing. Only a complete demolition of these toxic systems can form the basis for a fair and sustainable planet, with or without humans in the picture.

The Forgotten Crisis

The most likely, palpable scenario, and the one which few want to entertain, is that by the time thousands die daily from the climate crisis, there will be too much hunger, war and lack of funds available for reform to even remember what the climate crisis was in the first place, who the Thing was, and how we got to this inferno. Everyone will be busy trying to find food or shelter from floods and heatwaves. It will be a time of panic, migration, isolationism, fascism and self-preservation, rather than collective solutions. As climate and the social situation deteriorate simultaneously, events are much more likely to take a natural turn towards a downward spiral of societal collapse, mirroring the chain reaction events which happen in any complex natural ecosystem full of delicate interdependencies.

Frighteningly, the Thing may still survive this collapse, albeit heavily injured. It will continue to find new ways to parasitize and monetize any last remaining resources, which will be highly valuable and therefore profitable, given their tremendous scarcity at that point. Necrocapitalism is like a wildfire. As brilliant and vigorous as it may be in the beginning, it soon has to search for a new place to burn - leaving behind only tumbleweeds to aimlessly patrol over a silent cemetery of extinction. But the embers still burn, quietly. They're always there, awaiting any new green growth which will help them turn again into a blaze.

Provided a nuclear holocaust has not rendered the planet completely uninhabitable, pockets of local economies who have rejected the Thing may exist within a wider framework of a global fascist tech dystopia, which has further emboldened the Thing via artificial intelligence assisted by smart surveillance. New high-tech tools of manipulation will find easy, fertile ground in the public's panic and desperation, allowing a new, even more ruthless version of the Thing to generate completely novel and innovative ways of creating and then monetizing public discontent. The Unhappiness Machine will become the Desperation Machine. The wider public's realisation that we are now past the peak of our species, will be the single biggest money maker post-collapse for politicians and corporations alike - bringing the psychonomy into a new, even more dystopian era in a much more poor and unstable planet.

"Hello, you are caller number 91. Our services may be slower than usual due to heavy disruption from the collapse of global industrial civilisation. But do bear with us please, one of our automated assistants should be with you shortly"

Invisible Dystopias

Some of these scenarios may be too bleak for anyone to consider, and too distant from current reality to be able to anticipate, and plan for. But they are not fantasies and they are certainly not impossible. They are highly likely, and many would argue that they have actually already come true or are in the process of materializing as we speak. All dystopias, including our current one, have a skillful way of making themselves invisible, by eventually become the "new normal": a tolerable form of pain, one which no one would ever dare describe as a "dystopia" - especially if this is the only reality they have ever known.

Dystopias are not reserved for the future, or for science fiction. They are all around us, right now, today. Throughout the ages, it has been easy for human societies to easily convince the average citizen that, the nightmare dystopia they may be living in, is in fact a modern paradise beyond their wildest dreams. The purpose of the media has always been to make unbearable dystopias appear palatable, products appear useful, and corrupt leaders appear honest. The media are nothing but the PR machine of our psychonomy, always securing a generous cut from its proceeds.

Information Pandemics

Society has become a drug addict trapped in its own hallucinations, which are essential in order to survive this dystopia. We have built a civilisation and self-affirming psychonomy which do everything in their power to maintain our delusion that this party will go on forever. The media machine of the farm, which is about to be outsourced to the Thing through AI-generated news content, has already become almost fully automated and intelligent. AI trolls funded by the business interests of the Thing are already skewing and distorting any meaningful online conversation through engineered news, polarization, deep fakes, microtargetting and "shitposting". This is not simply a threat to democracy. It is a threat to reality.

This clever game is increasingly falling out of human control. The creation and dissemination of toxic fake news is a artform which we engineered, nurtured and experimented with for hundreds of years. Now everything that we have learned about human manipulation is being imbued into next generation marketing algorithms. Manual marketing and propaganda are dead. They are a harmless, benign version in comparison to what is coming. As political marketing fully interfaces with the technology which has been at the forefront of consumatron advertising for decades, it rapidly gives way to a new marketing brain which can guess which party we affiliate with, based on which shoes we bought. It knows each and every one of us better than we know ourselves, from just a few pieces of our digital footprint.

This is not simply marketing on steroids. This is not religion. This is an algorithm which has the power to convert even the smartest human into a member of the most bizarre cult, if it wants to. It is a deep fake algorithm which will soon be able to video call you, impersonate your mom, and ask you for ransom. The barrier between what is real and what is not, is about to become ever more hazy and catastrophically precarious.

We are in the process of creating an autonomous, living being, a bug which can increasingly think and replicate on its own. We are unleashing this bug on an already gullible and increasingly scared population, leaving it to decide which type of information pandemic it wants to create, where, and when just as climate crisis calamities hit specific spots in the world. As these algorithms become increasingly intelligent, able to reverse-engineer an entire propaganda based on the desired result (or government), the million-dollar question is: who is more dangerous: the algorithms as they eventually become autonomous, or the humans themselves, who are still largely in charge of developing and guiding these algorithms?

Brain Inundation

We may think that we are simply slaves to our CO_2-emitting consumerism, but in reality we are slaves to something much more sinister, and increasingly more intelligent: the Thing is a web of manipulation which spans the corporate interests of the psychonomy, political power structures, and popular culture narratives which the human herd has always needed, and looked up to for guidance. Almost every piece of stimulus we are exposed to is being reverse-engineered with specific outcomes in mind. As AI is increasingly brought in to optimize and supercharge this manipulation, what was once a "process" is now literally becoming a being, a "Thing". We have been witnessing the emergence of a hyper-mutational, adaptive and self-learning form of digital, sentient capitalism which knows us even better than ourselves - and which is increasingly able to censor every last bit of truth that remains, literally turning black into white with terrifying ease.

This necrocapitalist political system, now operated by the Thing, is a self-endorsing digital fascism which can shut down all dissent that may pose a threat to its financial bottom line: not by force, but by misinformation. This is especially easy to achieve, using the old-fashioned tried and tested method: control the sources of information. The new propaganda machine knows how to get on top of the attention economy, and turn it into the fascism of distraction. This is not brainwashing. It is brain inundation to the extent that reality becomes such a minority opinion, it is deemed as conspiracy theory.

The Consumatron Theme Park

Necrocapitalism manages to hide its dark agenda behind the most colourful, mesmerizing shopfront: an endless theme park of consumerism, where our physical senses succumb to the lights, the smells, the sounds, the promises of a better "life". "Retail therapy" as it is called, is a euphemism for the intravenous narcotics of consumerism which numb the pain of living in a sick society: the rent we struggle to pay, the life lost sitting in traffic, the boss who just had a go at us for no reason just half an hour ago. The psychonomy has no choice but to become even more controlling and oppressive, as 8 billion people fight over dwindling resources. This will require an ever more cunning, hypnotising and sinister unhappiness machine of consumerism.

But this shopfront, even though completely artificial, is what feels most vividly real to the vast majority of us: work, coffee, shopping, ice cream, a walk in the park, a dinner in the city, a doctor's appointment. Everything is working like clockwork, down to the last detail. We feel safe, secure, and tranquilized by all the busyness in our lives, the ever increasing list of things that we have to do to survive within this system. If nothing else, we have the excuse of being too busy to wake up from our consumatron coma. Besides, everyone else is doing exactly the same. Surely all of this cannot just "collapse"?

We happily accept this manufactured normality which has been carefully drawn and coloured-in by our favourite brands - and we believe all of it, every single bit of it, because we desperately want to feel reassured. We are hostage to the sense of safety and stability that we must secure no matter what, refusing to even entertain the thought that maybe this colourful theme park is built on top of a cemetery populated with the graves of everything and everyone who had to die in the process of building all the fun rides and hot dog stands. Maybe the cemetery is set on top of a dark swamp, ready to swallow and recycle everything as the ground becomes too heavy to hold the jenga towers of this civilisation.

Necrocapitalism always does its very best to make sure that we only see what's on the surface of the swamp, like a car salesman about to rip us off. We only see a freshly painted car. We never see the ugly mechanics of the system that lies under the hood of this necrocapitalist vehicle, and the nasty fuel it runs on. If we were to open the engine and take a look, we would see a rusty, overheating pile of junk ready to explode. We would see natural destruction, climate catastrophe, extinction and exploitation, the real drivers behind this beautifully illuminated, ephemeral theme park. The quicksand is getting hungry.

Living And Dying In The
Consumatron Zoo

Like with any commercial zoo, the visitors' brochure always shows happy animals delightfully roaming about in their confined, carefully curated cages, occasionally interacting gleefully with both the staff and the public. They are carefully photoshopped to look like animals who have chosen their "stardom": they love the attention and the spotlight, because all they ever wanted was to become social media celebrities. Besides, assuming the celebrity role was for them the least that they could do for their masters, as a thank you for all the free food they receive: they have been "cared for", given everything that they needed in order to survive in their tiny prison. Not because someone actually cares for them, but because they need to look healthy and happy for their next photoshoot. Above all, because they simply can't die. This would be bad publicity. They need to be maintained as they are, like necrocapitalist objects in a museum display case, bar the occasional dusting. Some of them have been born inside this prison, living their entire lives knowing that their purpose is to be props in a movie set. They are living to survive, not to exist, and do not know the difference between the two, simply because they have never experienced any version of reality other than the zoo.

The visitors of the zoo think that they are "the free ones". But they are living in a zoo themselves, constantly made to feel that they should be thankful to the psychonomy for all that it provides them with. They should be thankful, rather than resentful.

Both the visitors and the zoo animals have been defrauded. But they are unlikely to revolt. Only in extremely rare moments in history does the showy shopfront of the system briefly collapse, momentarily revealing all the ugliness, exploitation and despair, in all of its naked grotesqueness. Speechless, the people and animals are for the first time able to witness what lies behind the curtain. But before they can take a good look at this Ground Zero long enough to begin to process what they are seeing, a brand new curtain is drawn over the ghastly reality they've only had a brief glimpse of. The psychonomy's engineers are out in full force, repairing the glitch.

Phew. It must have been a hallucination, as everyone returns to their roles. The crazy colourful lights come back up, the carousel begins to spin, the music starts again right from where it had left off. There is no reason to wonder, not for a second, whether all of this theme park is real or not. How can it be fake when it is a glimmering heaven? So colourful, so tasty, so tangible? As long as people take their daily prescription of affirmations and entertainment drugs which the Thing generously provides, all of us, humans and animals, are living in a happy zoo, and a perfectly "normal" world. As long as we trust the Thing to run our lives and provide us with reassurance and protection, we are the happy algae locked inside this coral prison.

It takes immense vision, not to mention courage, for the few brave ones amongst us to wake up from our manufactured happiness in the necrocapitalist matrix, knowing already that the minute we do this we will become immediately depressed. How many of us wake up on a Monday, look outside our window and think: "What have we done to this world? What have we done to ourselves?" Even fewer will ever muster the motivation to think: "today I'm gonna drink my coffee, and then start a revolution against this system". They are more likely to smoke a cigarette then jump out the window.

Necrocapitalism vs the EoT

Humanity has, rather unconsciously, decided to engage in a futile war with the entire planet. Earth's biggest weapon against us is the climate, directed by an intelligence network I refer to as the EoT - the Earthnet of Things. The war at large is between the EoT, a sentient system which obeys physics and science, and the Thing, which does not. Humans are caught in the middle of this struggle between two Goliaths. Gaia will use the EoT to bring death, hunger, viruses, locusts, tornadoes, droughts, floods and hurricanes at times and in places never thought possible, in the hope of cutting down to size the malaise of necrocapitalism.

Humans may have invented consumerism, but Earth is the ultimate consumer. It can consume, recycle and reuse almost anything and everything - including entire human civilisations.

THE DREAM THAT HUMANITY IS
UNABLE TO WAKE UP FROM

The Mind Prison

Zen Buddhists often talk about something which may sound counter-intuitive, but is actually most profound: "The mind is a prison". According to this concept, all of us can become consumed by our own thoughts, preoccupied by them so intensely to the point where we become hijacked, ceasing to pay attention to real events and stimuli from the outer physical environment. We begin to alternate between the real world, and this made-up world inside of our thoughts, which our mind prison has constructed. As we spend more and more of our time in the latter, it begins to feel real, while at the same time the real world begins to fade, becoming a mere version of the world inside our mind prison.

In time, it can become difficult to distinguish between the two worlds, and to be able to register correctly whether we are in one world or the other, at any given point in time: the mind prison of our thoughts on one hand, or the real world, where real people live and die and real events occur. By living in this parallel universe, we can easily fall into a precarious state of unconsciousness whereby, although we may be able to perform all of our usual daily routine functions, we have lost cognition of everything real happening around us. We can begin to miss out on critical events which are outside of our normal routine, even as they unfold in broad daylight. Events which, had we been awake, we could have had a personal influence on.

Although this mental state may sound terrifying, it is more common than it sounds, and it does explain much of the tunnel vision, denial, ignorance, dogmatism and prejudice which have plagued humanity over the ages. The mind prison exists because it serves a purpose: it is a type of mental shortcut, a "safe" room to inhabit as we take shelter from an uncomfortable reality. It is incredibly efficient and convenient for us to place our brain on autopilot, and only use it for the familiar tasks critical to our survival - ignoring the more unusual, less front-of-mind, "big picture" items which require not only awareness, but analysis, processing and critique. These last three brain functions require a good grounding in the present, and this can only happen outside of the mind prison.

Desensitized To Reality

By spending too much time within our confined mind prison, we can easily become bystanders in our own world. Torn between multiple "realities" and multiple narratives, we may choose the safe option and become simple observers, treating the real world in the same way that we treat our inner "constructed" world: it becomes a series of thoughts and images that come and go, just like a movie or video game. Whereas we used to be able to tell the video game apart from the real world, everything now is the video game.

The mind prison is nothing but an endless library of video games and potential scenarios. Every time we are preoccupied with our professional image, our personal identity, the past or the future, the result is likely to be the same: we are entering a world that only exists in our head. As the scenarios multiply, assisted through copious exposure to stereotypes enforced by marketing and propaganda, we eventually shut down. We have been desensitized to reality, becoming passive viewers who only get up from the couch to make more popcorn.

The mind prison can be a creative space, but it can also become a trap. Although imagination is a useful skill, excessive rumination can lead to stress and other psychoses. But most importantly, it leads to an inability to stay in the present, see it for what it is, and assign it the importance and level of attention that it deserves. Given that the mind prison struggles to access reality and the sound evidence of real-time facts, it can be susceptible to corruption. The mind prison is indeed a prison, because it locks us out of the present. We end up living in the past or the future, which disables us from taking action right now. It is much like in a dream, where you try to run, only to find that there is no ground beneath you to run on.

Sleepwalking Into The Unknown

Living in the mind prison is increasingly the dominant way in which humans use their brain, and for many of us, the main place where we dwell for much of our time. The consequences of spending so much time in the virtual space of this never-ending dream are disastrous. By not being able to stay in the present, we cannot see the world in its true colors. The more we neglect the real world which lies outside of our mind prison, the more it deteriorates. If and when we ever wake up, this world may have already become a nightmare, and it won't be virtual this time.

Living in the mind prison is akin to sleepwalking: there is a top-level, rudimentary awareness which allows the sleepwalker to avoid bumping into familiar objects while able to visit certain places, even do some basic tasks. But make no mistake: they are on full autopilot, following a pre-programmed script which is in their head, not in the objective reality. The sleepwalker keeps a mental map of what their house interior looks like, and this is what they go by. Change the furniture around, and they are likely to bump into objects. They may assume that they are sleepwalking themselves to the kitchen of their house, but the kitchen might as well be on fire and they wouldn't even notice. The kitchen being on fire is a piece of information which the sleepwalker is simply unable to register. It lies outside of their internal programming.

Those of us consumed by our mind prison can therefore sometimes behave like sleepwalkers, having completely checked out of the reality continuously unfolding around us. The paradox of the mind prison is that it exemplifies how our own brain can make us dumb: ironically, the advanced brainpower of humans means that they are arguably much more susceptible to their own thoughts, and therefore to the influence of the mind prison. Our brains are very effective at resisting the real world, and constructing their own realities.

Heroes, Villains, and Religions

Over the millennia, the human mind prison has fabricated entire religions in order to justify its actions, manipulate itself and others, or simply find "safe" explanations for things it did not understand. In their most primal incarnation, these narratives were initially conjured up to attribute a certain weather pattern or natural event to a personified causative force, such as a god. In time, the narratives matured into elaborate mythologies with a full cast of characters, and the mythologies eventually became religions, which were another beast altogether: while still very much narrative-based at their core, they had now been leveraged into powerful tools of social control and centralization of authority by the nascent necrocapitalist psychonomy. However different their motives may have been, in the end all of these narratives, mythologies and religions had the same origin: they were born out of the imagination engine of the mind prison, as it created more and more safe mental havens for humans to shelter in. Their objective was one: to control public opinion, and ensure people continued to serve the psychonomy in order to maintain the existing power structure.

In our desperation to create these fake, safe spaces within our brain, many of our narratives curiously began to resemble each other: they seemed to always aim to attribute responsibility to fictional characters. Heroes and villains, whether they were gods, semi-gods or actual historical humans who were idealized over the ages, became essential elements of whatever narrative we invented. The goal of these characters was to take responsibility away from us, so that we don't have to shoulder any blame. Common across cultures are stories of either a villain (e.g. Eve, Prometheus) who made a tragic error and cursed all future generations, or a hero who redeemed all future generations, sometimes explicitly (and bizarrely) dying for the sins of future people who they had never met. Another very popular narrative, often encountered across cultures, involves a hero accidentally setting the foundations of an entire new country. Such is the simplification and manipulation that our mind prison strives for, that we like to attribute the existence of entire countries to a single person. The simpler the narrative, the more resonant it will be amongst the gullible masses who crave for belonging, an identity, any safe mind prison they can keep in their back pocket which they can retreat to.

Fear as a Weapon

With each of these narratives, the mind prison managed to reassure us, and protect us, from any personal responsibility or blame. This relinquishing of control to the "blame vessel" of the hero or villain was not only reassuring. It was deliberate and manipulative. Given that the least we could do was to return the favour to the hero who died for us, or the pioneer who founded our country, in return we would now have to abide, from now and until eternity, by all the rules of the necrocapitalist economy. Those who disobeyed the rules and actually took initiative and responsibility for their own actions and decisions, would become the villains in the narrative - the bad people who would now shoulder actual blame, and for this reason, enter a never-ending purgatory: hell.

Voila. Modern, fear-based human society was born.

These various religious rules were of course put in place to maintain expansionist population policies, keep the status quo in place, and make the rich and powerful even more rich and powerful. Religion was really a cover up for executing necrocapitalist economic policy. And our mind prison had been central to this: it catered to our deepest fears and concerns using the most irresistible narratives, duly serving the interests of growth economics, and the voracious power structures which delivered them.

Truth, Rewritten

It is worth realising the corrosive power of the mind prison: the truth is not simply adjusted or distorted in order to fit the events. It is completely rewritten. As far as the sleepwalker is concerned, the kitchen was never on fire.

Humans have been using mental maps, religions and narratives for thousands of years to simplify their lives, as much as these very tools turn them into sleepwalkers. Today, thousands of years after our religions were formed, we still seem to be much better at remembering scenes from the Bible which supposedly happened in the very distant past, than the modern, Biblical catastrophes of the climate and ecological Armagedon our generation is bearing witness to with its own eyes, right here right now. This is because narratives, however fake, are always much more powerful than reality, weather forecasts or climate scientists appearing in the news. Narratives are cathartic: they attribute blame, and secure closure. These stories are addictive, because we want so badly to believe in them. Our civilization has been constructing mind prisons within mind prisons almost since its inception. Most of our narratives are fictional, surreal and half-baked. Yet they have been so corrosive that they have managed to stick to our brains, passed down from generation to generation, forming a significant part of our "cultural traditions".

Emotional Censorship

The mind prison is a barrier to truth, because it is capable of disabling our natural sensing systems. We are much more capable than other species to override cues from our hormones and instincts, which however are vital, visceral responses to the real world, and which often serve as important alerts and warnings. These hormonal responses are the source of much of our emotional intelligence and spiritual compass, our "heart" so to speak.

Our social system plays a crucial role in damping down all of our emotions, our "truth", as this has always been an objective of the psychonomy. There is an ultimate economic and political motive behind not only controlling people's emotions, but disabling people's ability to know how they are feeling, and what they are feeling. This way, people lose their inner compass. This is what the psychonomic farm wants, so that the human cattle literally cannot find their way out.

Our leaders of course do not want people who have found their inner truth, because these people are more likely than others to be happy and satisfied, and cannot be as effectively manipulated based on their apprehensions. It is better for our leaders if we are all unsettled, terrorised and lost, with many raw, unprocessed and unresolved emotions inside of us which are much easier to weaponize. These unprocessed emotions sit in the back of our minds like forgotten radioactive dump sites, waiting for the right propaganda to hijack them and provide them with a toxic outlet. They are unleashed as weapons, directed to whoever and wherever the mind prison chooses.

Scared and confused people are much, much easier to manipulate. They are routinely assisted by the politicians, religions or other movements to resolve their emotions not through healing, but through anger and polarization which are passively-agressively expressed at the voting booth. The reason why our religion and society classified much of our emotional world as "taboo" was so that emotions are never properly processed and resolved, and become weapons instead. We have been discouraged from feeling, from living many of our emotions, exactly because of how powerful, honest, and genuine they are, and because they bring us in contact with the world, with ourselves, and with our inner truth. Emotions had to become "taboos", so that people are not able to "own" themselves at a deeper level. Instead, they have surrendered ownership to those who will come and interpret their emotions for them. Anyone who has fallen out of touch with how they are feeling, and what they are feeling at any given point, is already a slave.

The Weaponized, Socialized Mind Prison

What these religions and centers of power did next, was to assume the role of "family psychologist", telling us with new, fantastical narratives, how to interpret, process, and act on our raw emotions and fears. They processed these emotions on our behalf, interpreting them for us and telling us how to live our lives, who to have sex with, what is acceptable and what isn't, all for the ultimate purpose of maintaining the prevailing power and economic structures.

Despite all the benefits of living within a society, it is important to recognise that social organisation is a means of emotional suffocation. This has been one of the disadvantages of large, organized societies. Although humans need a society for their survival, group dynamics can lead to herd behaviors which extinguish the healthy parts of our ego and convert individuals to inanimate objects within the greater social purgatory. This happens to an extent even within countercultures and marginalised groups, and even within anarchy movements who claim to have rejected society. The tendency within any group is for rules, regulations, and leaders to spontaneously emerge. Power is like a multi-headed, regenerating beast: you can try and "eat the rich", or "send the elites to prison", but more of them will emerge out of nowhere, literally overnight.

The fictional Cyborg race in Star Trek is a prophetic vision of what is happening to humanity today at the macro social level: despite being more "connected" than ever before with each other, sometimes we literally cannot see in front of us. All "manual controls" have been disabled. We live in our brains and apps, but also increasingly in one, shared brain that makes decisions for us by narrowing our options down to a rudimentary list. Just like the Cyborgs, our vision has atrophied, because we do not need it anymore. We have forgotten how to use it, as images of the new, virtual world are served ready for us from the mass media, telling us exactly who we are, where we are, what we are seeing, and how we should feel about it.

Safe and Asleep

Most of us are quick to find safety in simply following others' example in what we do or think. We blindly place our trust in the majority of an otherwise collective unconsciousness of sheep, who are in the end all following each other in a circle. Obstructing us from accessing our own, inbuilt, vast emotional reservoir, the mind prison takes over, assisted by the narratives coming from organized power. Removed from our own personal truth, each of us finds shelter in the mind prison which makes us feel the most secure.

We are already living in the age when very few of us can recognize or remember what a "free-range", free-thinking human was: probably an artist, terrorist, or someone who just forgot to recite their system-prescribed affirmations in the morning, and suddenly woke up to realise that they are living in the necrocapitalist matrix. It would seem that these people, these revolutionaries, are becoming increasingly rare in an ever more constrictive, controlling and suffocating psychonomic society.

Over the past century, the various channels of propaganda, political marketing machines and consumatron advertising agencies which build and curate our various mind prisons, have perfected their science of representing, maintaining and reinforcing the most backwards, oppressive and exploitative forces in our society. Critics often complain about how corrupt the media is, how they "fail" to represent news accurately, e.g. when it comes to the climate crisis. I find this view incredibly naive. The role of the media is not to be representative, democratic, or impartial. The role of the media, since its inception, has always been to make dystopias look like a walk in the park, and leaders appear truthful - and useful. Along with religion, the media is part of the PR machine of the psychonomy. We should not expect it to be fair, impartial, or democratic, as long as there is always someone in the background handpicking, distorting, and reworking "the news".

The world that the media have created inside of our brains is a monetisable commodity which they fully control, exploit and manipulate. The walls of our otherwise dark, cold and damp mind prison are covered with holograms of windows looking out into open countryside, in order to give us the false impression that we are free – and that in fact, we can escape from the farm any time we want to. The holographic walls of the prison can change at any point to accommodate new hallucinations, new messages and "truths" that the system needs to disseminate.

Keep Calm and Keep Feeding the Algorithm

Whoever manages to control this central brain we all receive our cues from, succeeds in controlling us. Whereas previously this role was mainly filled in exclusively by religious narratives, today it has become much more sophisticated, with the advent of elaborate marketing and propaganda which can manipulate us in much more subtle, sinister and deeply subconscious ways which easily overcome our detection. The truth is constantly being re-written, as well as increasingly customized for each and every one of us individually, via the algorithmic microtargeting of consumatrons with products, news and campaigns tailored to our most gullible senses.

The Thing knows us better than ourselves. Just like the butterfly collector, it has measured us, classified us, arranged us by size, then cleverly targeted us with customised messages coming from virtual humans: human-like bots who have been created for one-off interactions, just to have a conversation with us. This is the dawning of the algorithmocracy: a new form of machine-mediated political system whereby the use of extremely sophisticated algorithms is employed to manipulate public opinion, and essentially control power. The algorithms are trained on psychology and marketing data, are able to continuously self-learn using the consumatrons' digital footprint, personify themselves as human-like bots, and customize their interaction on a bot-to-human level in order to achieve specific manipulation objectives which require very minimal human input or supervision.

Algorithmocracy of course, has the potential to become entirely machine-owned and operated. While for the time being the patrons of this algorithmocracy continue to be the economic oligarchs, they are increasingly outsourcing our manipulation to entities which are not even biological: artificial intelligence programs proficient in human psychology and behaviour, able to know us and "type" us instantly. It has become incredibly easy to create fake news targeted to each and every one of us individually, a process so efficiently optimized through machine-learning that it enables truth to be literally re-written and curated in the most life-like, high-fidelity and convincing execution. We are only just about cracking the door open to this terrifying revolution where machines will be able to manipulate us as easily as it is for humans to inhale and exhale. Automated AI bots can already enter online human-to-human conversations and disrupt, distort, misinform and misguide, pretending to be human. They do so by crowding-out other opinions to the point where a "credible majority" of the fake opinion is established. It is extremely easy.

Supermarketization of News

When it comes to the unfolding climate Armagedon, this increasingly sentient mass media entity has managed to create a special place within our mind prison where we can feel deceptively safe and reassured: where the climate crisis is real on one hand, but manageable and reversible, on the other. As always, the goal is for us to become passive observers, while the necrocapitalist machine continues to destroy whatever is left of this planet. Please have your credit cards ready to accelerate the collapse.

Key to this expanding mind prison is the very way in which we interact with the news - that is, if we ever care to watch them. We can only really see what has been carefully pre-selected and put in front of us within the images of the mind prison. In functional terms, news has merged with entertainment, so that it can become another product for the consumatrons - given that most consumatrons now only understand our world through products, brands and entertainment. News has now essentially ceased to represent information: it has become an entertainment product, a consumable. This means that our role as a media consumatron is confined to bringing out the popcorn and observing passively, as opposed to critiquing, debating, forming an opinion and even taking action and responsibility in response to "the news".

The Popcorn Will Be Burnt

The result, when it comes to climate change and the ecological apocalypse, is that what used to be real has now become a Hollywood movie which our prison brain falsely thinks it can switch off, or simply change the channel to Planet B. The ongoing destruction of the planet is nothing but a reality show we are observing from a safe distance live on our screens, sitting in our couches, without any conscious sense of the significance of what we are actually watching, of the fact that structures of the planet which have been around for millions of years like glaciers, ancient forests, the Great Barrier Reef, the entire insect kingdom, are being wiped out of existence. Forever.

All of this is happening in the real world, not in an entertainment program - yet it seems light years away from the four LCD walls of the mind prison. And despite the fact that we are conscious of what we are seeing on the news, in behavioral terms it would appear that our brain simply does not register this information as "real" anymore - because it has begun to uncouple itself from physical reality. The high-resolution, deep fake "truths" which the system creates on the other hand, appear much more real.

It is likely that we became blind a long, long time ago. This was engineered to benefit necrocapitalism and the psychonomy, the machines which need to constantly weaponise and monetise our mind prison. Some of us know very well that we are trapped in our zombie dream: our role as a citizen has long ago been reduced to simply observing, with the sole purpose of being exposed to product advertisements in-between the "news" headlines.

Our role is not to be an active member of society anymore, because this would not suit the politicians, and it would be an unwelcome distraction from bringing out the credit card to buy stuff advertised while we "read" the news. Being an active citizen is perceived as a threat by the psychonomy. Our preferred, assigned role is to be a consumatron whose only problem is that the popcorn is beginning to taste like ash.

The Missed Revolution

Revolutions tend to break out only when people genuinely feel that the system which is oppressing them is so harsh and unbearable, that they would rather take the risk of revolting than stay put. For this to happen, their current regime needs to feel truly life-threatening.

We have yet to reach this point today, given that the mind prison can blunt and minimize any threat which appears in our rear-view mirror. The current system of oppression is a departure from previous regimes, which complicates the possibility of creating the conditions for the uprising that we desperately need. Rather than oppressing us, the system cleverly manipulates us so that we are the ones oppressing ourselves: we are the ones running after the money, the consumer products, desperately trying to make our life match our instagram feed. We are the ones who have stopped watching the news, and switched to funny cat videos.

There may not be a revolution in the near term, simply because if there ever was one, it would need to be against our own mind prison. Today's humans are not simply brainwashed. They are programmed to the point where they have become emotionless consumatrons exclusively preoccupied with themselves. Necrocapitalism has achieved something tremendous: to normalise an extreme form of narcissism in all of us, one which absorbs all of our energy and renders us passive, emotionless and devoid of ethics or a conscience. Almost everything we do in our daily life is to attain income and cater to the many needs that our necrocapitalist dystopia has implanted in us. There is barely any time or space for an average human to contemplate the meaning of their existence, to even question where this civilization is heading, simply because we have surrendered all the big existential questions to the big brother watching over us. And this is exactly what the CO2-emitting machine of necrocapitalism wants: to keep us distracted while it finishes off whatever natural resources remain on this planet - before finishing off itself.

The Rise of Human Ultra-Supremacy

We live in a digital farm, our every activity and endeavor monetized for profit in order to feed the psychonomy. This is why the system has strived to convert us to ultra-narcissists. The more we consume, the better. At every step of the way the digital mind prison does its best to minimize potential panic, and prevent us from waking up: if it is too hot outside, the sensors inside the farm will pick up our mood and placate us with made-up truths, new villains and heros, or new products, while cranking up the air-conditioning to reassure us that the planet will be just fine.

The mind prison comes with its own in-built censorship and propaganda machine: it is able to apply context and framing around any situation to defuse it, minimize it, normalize it, deny it and neatly package it at the very back of our brain so that we can carry on with "more important business".

But no hologram, LCD screen or other digital projection technology will ever simulate or recreate the world that we are leaving behind, and which we are making extinct. Images and memories of the ecosystems we destroy vanish forever, along with the life forms that lived in them. Future humans, if they exist, may try to imagine through virtual reality what it was like to walk barefoot on the grass of a wild meadow surrounded by flowers and buzzing insects, or picking fruit from a tree. They will never experience the scents, the sound of grass in the wind, the sun on their face. They won't even know what these things are. And yet, they will be provided with an endless, infinite menu of virtual simulations, customised to their personal preferences. That is, if humanity ever survives to attain this dystopian, next-level consumatronic farm state.

Reality Is Dead

Decades of this hyper-narcissistic programming have made modern humans progressively less curious and increasingly apathetic about what is happening to the planet, and ever more shallow and self-centered. This means that our relationship with reality is dysfunctional to say the least. Living within our mind prison, we are not able to register real events, even as they happen in front of our screen. These events may as well be a movie or other form of entertainment. As we witness the destruction of our world, our reaction is exactly the same as watching the movie Independence Day, or similar: all of this is not real, and it will pass when the movie is over. The irony of course is that the only thing palpably real anymore is this collapsing planet - everything else is concocted by our mind prison. Truth is synthetic. Happiness is manufactured. Work is mostly bullshit jobs, and even "meaningful meaning" is a commodity, bought and sold by the most absurd concept: money. Meanwhile, there is an important message: "We interrupt our colourful coverage of the Global Collapse for a very short Chipotle commercial".

While climate activists continue to raise the issue of lack of coverage of the climate catastrophe in the news, more coverage won't necessarily help. It is likely to result in more desensitisation, hypernormalisation, sleep, conditioning and complacency as the farm's digital sensors defend their version of the truth. Any coverage of our collapsing climate and ecosystems will be positioned by the nitrous media as light entertainment in between fast-food commercials. The more images our brain is saturated with, whether real or fake, the more we could get sucked into the black hole of fake hyper-reality that the prison brain is. We may have installed eyes, ears, cameras and satellites all over Earth's surface - but we still remain utterly blind to the greed that has suffocated this planet, choking all life to extinction.

It is an unsettling paradox that the prison brain gets stronger, not weaker, the more imagery it absorbs. Meanwhile, our active brain functions become more and more weakened.

Waking Up From The Dream

Re-establishing consciousness is the first step in leaving the mind prison. As with any muscle or organ of the body, the human brain needs regular exercise, but not within the prison. It should involve engaging with the world, with other humans, as well as with our forgotten emotions. Scrolling through social media, playing games on the smartphone and reading "opinions" in the news without stopping to form our own opinion does not count as conscious brain exercise. Escaping the mind prison takes effort, which begins with understanding how the necrocapitalist system has conspired against us. We can begin to recognise the passive relationship we have come to have with information, our decreasing ability to interact with real humans in live debates, and our separation from the physical and natural world where real events take place. This conscious effort is difficult, when most of us have been consciously trained to become unconscious.

As this sleepwalking civilization walks through the desert towards its conclusion, it may feel on multiple occasions that its judgement is failing, and that it should turn around. But the mirages projected out into the distance by the farm will be temptingly reassuring. Will enough of us be able to recognize them?

The world is falling deeper into sleep as the fog of misinformation thickens. Digital debris increasingly saturates the space between our souls, suffocating the truth. We've lost sight of the exit door of the farm. As long as people are asleep and busy working the jobs which feed the very system responsible for our predicament, we are rapidly heading for an apocalyptic catastrophe which will end civilisation, life, and close down the farm for good, or turn it into a cannibalistic even more dystopian version. We are trapped inside a dream, and we are unable to wake up.

The global collapse of industrial civilisation is most likely to continue to be managed effectively by half-truths, green hopium and figments of new heroes and villains who will emerge to fill the gaps of our emotional abyss. What is likely to remain out of control however, and out of the news, is the climate and ecological apocalypse, and any hints into the future which our children may have hoped for.

I consider the absurd scenario quite possible that, the climate crisis will be completely forgotten in the very near future. World war, starvation, power cuts, migration and death will become far more important than what caused them all: the man-made climate catastrophe. Under a more favourable scenario, civilisational collapse may dramatically reduce emissions, temporarily end climate denialism, and dissolve the most toxic socioeconomic structures responsible for the planet's demise, allowing some of us to envisage new societies in the few habitable areas left on the planet. But if humans make it through this, eventually history is likely to repeat itself. Wherever there is "intelligence", there is a mind prison to match it.

THE NEVER, NEVER, NEVERLAND
OF DEGROWTH

The Fairy Tale Is Over

Those following the more pragmatic conversations on the topic know that, if there ever was a chance of keeping this planet habitable, it wouldn't be through solar panels and electric vehicles. These technologies would come at an incredible carbon and ecological cost, if they were ever to be deployed at the massive scale required to power 8 billion energy-hungry humans. The utopian myth of offsetting emissions while we continue to ramp up our energy use has stood the test of time, but only as a fairy tale. It was an irresistible, incredibly attractive fairy tale which would have allowed us to have our cake, and eat it as well. But it has miserably and spectacularly failed, as one after the other, renewable energy projects were only used as energy top-ups used to service an escalating energy demand, rather than replacing fossil fuel-generated energy. As a result of unchecked economic growth, population growth and toxic "green growth" of renewable technologies, carbon emissions as well as energy use continue to climb. In addition, renewable technologies themselves have come and continue to come at a tremendous carbon emissions and ecological destruction cost, simply as a result of their manufacturing and installation process. Scaling them up further will not solve the problem, in much the same way that adding more lanes to a highway does nothing to solve traffic issues in the long term. The math has been done, and the climbing emissions are there to prove it. The Green New Deal has already failed. The solution lies somewhere else.

The Fraud of Replacement Economics

We have failed emissions reduction targets because the more renewable energy we install, the more energy-hungry we become. Rather than managing the real issue, our ballooning energy use, we have chosen to replace one problem with another: replacing fossil fuel with renewable - but not sustainable - forms of energy. This follows a long history of replacement economics: the profitable yet deceptively effective approach of solving issues by replacing the technology, rather than addressing the issue itself. This manages to defer the issue into the future under the guise of negligible, temporary and incremental benefits - while leaving it unaddressed, and compounded by additional issues which come with the new, untested technology. We have done this many times before. Three glaring examples of replacement economics follow:

Over the past few decades our food industry replaced fats with industrially-made carbohydrates, under the pretense of tackling obesity and making "low fat products". Of course carbohydrates became even more addictive than fats, and obesity skyrocketed. The food industry had chosen to replace one ingredient with another, rather than tackle obesity itself, which is about how many calories people eat, how often, and how natural their food is, the latter affecting glycemic index among other factors. The consequences of replacement economics in the food industry have been criminally disastrous and continue to be to this day, as the obesity and diabetes epidemics gather pace and affect progressively younger age groups.

However, the replacement of fats with carbs in our food was an extremely profitable approach for the food industry, as they were able to create new, highly addictive foods made from cheap raw materials such as high fructose corn syrup, which increased revenues substantially. There was never any intention whatsoever by the food industry to address obesity. It was all about making people eat more, at less cost to the manufacturer. If the food industry really wanted to help, they would have made more natural foods, but they would lose consumers as these foods would be more expensive. Moreover, these foods would be far from addictive, so this would be an additional huge hit to their profits. By replacing one food technology with another, the food industry had failed to solve obesity, and further compounded it with many additional issues that have led to a massive social and public health problem which is far too complex to analyse here.

The second example of failed replacement economics is transportation policy: in order to address an increasing number of vehicles on the road, governments across the world have historically chosen to expand highway infrastructure, rather than provide incentives for people to travel less, own fewer cars, increase their use of public transportation, and a myriad other ways in which the real issue, our increased mobility, can be tackled. The famous line "one more lane will fix it" emerged to describe the common practice of adding one more lane to a highway in order to relieve traffic, only to find that within six months the traffic situation is back to square one, and even worse: the highway has become congested, saturated, blocked to a standstill, yet again.

Similarly, replacing fossil fuel-powered cars with electric vehicles does nothing to address the traffic issue, nor the carbon emissions issue. Electric vehicles may be more energy efficient and environmentally "friendly", but only once they are owned. Before that, and up to the big day when they end up at the car dealer to be sold, they have already amassed an incredible amount of carbon footprint, which is a result of all aspects of their manufacturing. Once these cars are dead, their batteries become an environmental disaster as well. There is still no effective, ecologically viable and sustainable way of recycling these batteries - a tiny detail which the "green" car manufacturers forgot to tell us when they were prompting us to save the planet by buying an electric vehicle. Ooops.

It is therefore ironic that these so-called "green" vehicles are a threat to the planet during their birth, as well as after their death. Only during their actual lifetime, as functioning cars, do they potentially offset some of the emissions of their manufacture and post-death processing. However, in our throw-away necrocapitalist society, they are much more likely to be thrown into the car cemetery way before they have even died and offset significant emissions, just so that the car owner can purchase the next most fashionable EV model.

Necrocapitalism always wins. All products, people and resources must die before their expiration. The sooner they do, the more profit is pocketed. And just as with the food industry example, replacing one technology with another, replacing one highway with another or one car technology with another, is a failed approach. It is however, extremely profitable.

Net Zero vs. Real Zero: The Myth Of Emissions Offsetting

And this brings us to how replacement economics has been playing out in the energy industry sector as a whole. It is perhaps the saddest example, especially since so many environmental activists have fallen for the myth that is the Green New Deal. Offsetting carbon emissions while continuing to pursue economic growth is an investor fairy tale, and the biggest lie of the Green New Deal. As with previous replacement models, the real issue, which is our escalating energy use and its corresponding emissions, has been ignored in order to make money from new, carbon-intensive technologies. While these new energy sources are indeed renewable, the technologies which deliver them are not sustainable, both ecologically and in terms of carbon emissions. The end result is more carbon emissions, which continue to feed the climate catastrophe. To put it very simply, there is no way of making the existence of 8 billion modern, industrial-age humans "sustainable" by any stretch of the imagination. There is no way of "canceling out" human impact on Earth by taking sustainable actions, when these humans are increasingly wasteful, energy-hungry, and multiplying. The only way of balancing out human presence is by doing the obvious: lessening our overall presence on this planet.

The only way of cancelling out emissions is by actually reducing emissions. This means a contraction of the entirety of human civilisation, and this is the only solution which actually obeys simple, quantitative algebra, as well as the physics of the ecosystem and the planet. Our algebra should not be about Net Zero emissions, which has miserably failed. It should be about Real Zero: a measurable, tangible, quantitative decrease in the toxic by-products of this decaying civilisation.

Demand Reduction Does Not Compute

Obviously, the issue is not the source of energy we use, fossil or renewable, neither is it the technology which we use to produce that energy. It is our energy demand itself, and we just don't seem to have any desire to reduce our usage. Neither do the investors of the Green New Deal, who just want to make money from the "green revolution". Necrocapitalism is fully and truly in charge of this green revolution, and the fossil fuel industry is already well on its way to be replaced by the renewable energy industrial complex. We have failed emissions reduction targets not only because renewable technologies are not sustainable as a whole, but because we are deploying these technologies in the most dirty, profit-motivated, necrocapitalist manner.

The replacement economics need to end. The unscrupulous renewable installations need to end, and the management of our energy demand needs to begin, if there is any chance in reducing overall emissions. While we terminate fossil fuels.

The "reduce vs replace" argument applies not only to our energy, but to every aspect of human civilisation responsible for overshoot. Rather than building more "stuff", we should be tearing down what already exists, which is already overburdening the planet. Only a major downsizing of our entire civilization would suffice to reduce not only our emissions, but all elements of overshoot which have crossed into red territory: food, water, biodiversity, soil, oceans to mention just a few. This is a polycrisis which can only be tackled by one solution: reduce, reduce, and reduce. Everything. We cannot maintain our current lifestyle, and we can certainly never have net zero emissions with a net 8 billion population of increasingly tech-dependent, energy-hungry humans.

It is clear that downsizing is long overdue on all fronts: emissions, population, ecological devastation. We have entered a precipitous age where we very quickly need to completely shift from spending our time and energy achieving, doing and building, to finding ways of undoing, simplifying and deconstructing many of our previous generations' so-called "accomplishments".

The Myth Of The Evil Oil Tycoon

Many prefer to simplify the problem by inventing villains, as we have done numerous times throughout our history. In this case, the villains are a handful of fossil fuel tycoons, and 100 or so corporations responsible for 71% of global emissions. They are villified over and over by climate activists who are naive enough to believe that the world consists of only good people and evil people, and that somehow the current society and our lifestyle could continue more or less unabated, provided we simply removed these people and their companies, and replaced them with solar panels, wind turbines and permaculture allotments.

Well, it turns out that there are 8 billion people dependent on these CEOs, their companies, and all of the products, energy and salaries that those emissions produce through all of the supporting (and supported) industries affiliated with fossil fuel. In this sense, almost all 8 billion of us are equally "evil" by being fully complicit - whether we like our role or not. Our entire modern lifestyle and consumatronic frenzy was built on the back of massively destructive industries which scaled up our exploitation of this planet, and made our population mushroom to 8 billion, almost overnight. Fossil fuel extraction is just one of many of these destructive industries. The problem is not limited to a handful of industries. The problem is the modern human, their lifestyle, all the goods and services which they have come to expect as part of their daily lives, and the sheer size of this population which is a topic that the environmental movement shrugs away in denial. The urge to breed is too strong to resist, even among those who know very well that their yet unborn children will be experiencing a living hell. Perhaps they will be experiencing this hell together with their children, much earlier than they previously expect.

Yes, the fossil fuel industry needs to end, but all eco-destructive industry needs to end as well. There are barely any eco-compliant industries on this planet, and this sadly includes the so-called renewable, but not sustainable, "green" energy industrial complex. The "clean industries" which the Green New Deal investors have fabricated simply do not exist. The inconvenient truth is that the real problem is the wasteful lifestyle of consumers, which requires the existence of such destructive industries in the first place. The problem is not fossil fuel CEOs. The problem is our civilisation: you, me, and them. All of us.

The Inconvenient Message
Of Downsizing

But of course, none of our politicians have the guts to tell us that, if emissions were to decrease at the rate they need to, the government would need to take our toys away. Instead, they promise us that we can continue to live wastefully, while they put up some wind turbines to "cancel it all out" - then tweet about it on their next social media political campaign, with lots of images of solar panels and wind turbines against beautiful blue skies with white cumulus clouds. The only change which a Green New Deal brings is that instead of our cash going to fossil fuel tycoons, it goes to the renewable industry tycoons. The "green" CO2 emitted by the manufacture, installation and construction which the Green New Deal plans would be no less harmful, and in fact no different chemically from the CO2 produced by fossil fuels. And if carried out, the last nail on the coffin of this planet.

The inconvenient message of downsizing is already being diluted, corrupted and weaponised by a new mind prison. The new buzzword to describe this economic contraction which we need is "degrowth", which is obviously an oxymoron. It was the best which its originators could do to create an intentionally jovial synonym for shrinking, downsizing, downscaling, without actually saying it. They were hoping that this new terminology would scare people less than "contraction". And they were right. Many of those naively and prematurely jumping on the increasingly fashionable bandwagon of degrowth don't even realise what contraction demands of us. They are claiming they can shrink this civilisation with the same confidence that the renewable energy industrial complex claimed many decades ago that it could shrink emissions. Hmmm. Not so fast.

Yes, contraction is indeed where we should be heading. But it will never happen if we put our trust into the usual suspects: investors, businessmen, and politicians. But most of all, if we assume that degrowth will be delivered by the current society, institutions, and psychonomic appparatus. It will take, if ever attainable, much more than that. It will take a new human race, with new values. Power and capital are overwhelmingly and disproportionately concentrated among those who insist that the Earth is greening, the planet is cooling, and population is decreasing - precisely because these people have everything to gain from the planet's destruction. As long as this continues to be the case, Earth is on course to become a wasteland with 100% accuracy.

History Is Against Us

The first, most obvious challenge of degrowth, which few of us realise, is that contraction has never been done, in fact not even attempted, ever. This is something we need to recognise in order to understand the magnitude of this challenge. Despite its short history, the human race has over the ages given rise to many different civilizations, every single one at some point facing the challenge of keeping up with its increasing demand for resources. Every time these resources became scarcer, there was very little strategy in place to conserve or manage them. In fact, no civilization has ever come even close to making the type of radical changes humanity needs to do today, in order to avert catastrophe. Like a stubborn patient refusing critical life-saving surgery, all of our civilizations eventually became sitting ducks, simply waiting for their collapse. They gave up, before even trying. This pathology needs to be dissected and analyzed.

Instead of becoming aware of the futility of servicing a continuously escalating demand for resources and energy, humanity has always preferred to expand its planetary smash-

and-grab operation in order to cater to its needs. We've always gone to significant lengths in securing the immediate supply of water, food and other resources. What all of our civilizations failed miserably in however, was questioning, predicting, managing, controlling and ultimately maintaining demand down to a sustainable level. On every single occasion, we preferred to spend now and save nothing for later, leaving future generations to fend for themselves in whatever world we would pass down to them. Nothing has changed since then. This model is still alive, only it is now on steroids, and with a much bigger demand base of 8 billion.

Our history demonstrates a terrifying pattern of repetition. Looking at how past human civilisations dealt with their growing pains, there are three main strategies by which they managed to mutate, evolve, and even overcome problems. Neither of these strategies, which I am about to explain, are available to us today. We can make the same mistakes as before, but this time we won't get away with them. The room for error is zero

At War with Anyone and Everyone

The first strategy we employed to address mounting shortages was war. Declining empires would manage to give themselves a few more hundred years of lifetime extension, by invading resource-rich neighbors with poor military capacity, as well as defenseless natural habitats home to millions of species. From ethnic cleansing to the annihilation of entire ecosystems, humans have used extinction as their preferred method to clear space, create opportunity, as well as clear their memory of any crimes they may have committed in the process. This violent and simple strategy is not available to us today, given that there are hardly any resource-rich areas on the planet which have not been exploited yet. If anything, the climate crisis is making us all poorer: impoverishing both the rich and developed world, and even making areas of the planet around the equator and beyond completely uninhabitable.

While this resource shortage is further exacerbated by our population size, war is simply not a solution for any nation today, for an additional reason: the economic system is too interconnected and globalized for any large power to benefit from conflict. We are not living in a collection of economies but one, large, global economy. A successful invader today stands to lose as much as they would gain from war. We all need each other, more than ever before, and in more ways than ever before. The magical age of empires, of slash and burn invasions, is firmly behind us.

Destroy and Move On

The second solution empires followed was to abandon their land altogether and move their administrative and economic center somewhere else within their territory: in other words, find some other place to exploit and destroy. The problem with this solution is that again, similar to war, it is not available to us anymore. Humans have overrun the planet, and there are very few untouched places left to exploit and destroy, a far cry from what would be needed to support an 8 billion-strong consumatron base which is ever more demanding and hungry. Those who advocate moving to another planet would also be bitterly disappointed: by the problems here on Earth will be too cataclysmic for any resources, industry and budget to exist for big projects such as space exploration. We are much more likely to destroy this planet way before we can even abandon it, and this is probably a blessing for any neighboring solar systems who would have been next in line to witness our appetite for destruction.

Technological Limits

The third strategy is technology. The agricultural and industrial revolutions were game changers for empires. Sadly, both of these strategies depended on resources which do not exist anymore. We have already farmed all the farmable land that is out there, and we have upscaled and automated industrial production to the point where both the manufacturing and supply chain systems are extremely sensitive to breakdown. Globalization, the complexity of advanced technology and its dependence on incredibly convoluted supply chains, simply so that it can exist, make our current world more prone to a sudden, global collapse than ever before. Even the ongoing information revolution, which may appear to be less resource-intensive, is actually incredibly energy-hungry. It requires vast quantities of electricity and rare earth metals to continue.

All technologies, however "clean" or "sustainable", have a voracious appetite for energy and resources, and an indelible footprint which can be catastrophically detrimental. It would be foolish to think that technology alone can achieve degrowth and "save" us, yet this is what many people simplistically assume. No industry, however new, innovative, efficient and "clean", can grow without a very significant input of raw materials, which undoubtedly has an impact on the planet.

The world is much more likely to be fighting with China in the near future for access to its rare earth metals, than be lucky enough to innovate and invent itself out of permanent recession. Besides, the technological future of humanity looks bleak if anything, given the increasing risk of humans being surpassed and/or terminated by a non-DNA based civilization evolving out of artificial intelligence. Our technology will continue to evolve, and assist us. But only if we learn to manage it. This is highly unlikely given that we are always much more keen to take the risk of technological disruption, in exchange for tantalizing yet temporary benefits.

Fearlessly Embracing Contraction

You will notice one common attribute across the main survival strategies of civilisations: they were all growth-based, which is of course why they would not be applicable today as part of an economic contraction plan. We cannot grow ourselves out of problems, when the problem itself is growth. What goes up must come down. Growth leads to collapse. As tragic and unlikely as civilizational collapse may sound, it has happened before to every single human civilization. It is the most natural, predictable and most probable outcome for an exponentially overgrown economic system, simply being brought back down to size by its own physics.

But scaling back our presence on the planet is an action contrary to everything our civilization has stood for, during the entirety of our history. Our skills, our intuition, our brain, are all geared towards "building" themselves out of problems: our knee-jerk reaction has always been the same: inventing, constructing, innovating technologies. This highlights the impossible conundrum we find ourselves in: how do we contract without "making stuff"? How can we learn to take a step back from time to time?

The answer would seem obvious, but somehow the message is not getting through to the right people. Many are still thinking of degrowth in "growth" terms, because they simply cannot process the concept of doing less. It is a taboo in our work-obsessed, growth-obsessed psychonomy. It is counter-intuitive not only to the mainstream business paradigm, but to our entire civilisation as we have come to know it since its beginnings. Denial of what real degrowth means is rife, pointing to challenges that have much less to do with our current economic system, and much more to do with our mindset. The concept of contraction simply does not seem to compute for most people. Hint: it is not meant to. We are not balancing books here, we are saving the planet. Contraction may not have immediate benefits to humans in terms of GDP or making the tycoons richer. It has benefits to the entire planet however, and its 8 million species, which includes humans. Economic contraction is the biggest investment humanity can make right now. It dwarfs any technological development or invention, because it safeguards the very existence of all of the above.

The Missing Champions of Degrowth

The growth-based strategies of the past managed to provide immediate boosts to the economy, and this is why there was never a shortage of champions and stakeholders who would go ahead and support these developments. Whether they were feudal landlords, slave traders, fossil-fuel oligarchs, clothing sweatshop CEOs or blood-thirsty warlords, they were always there: enthusiastic champions and investors, ready to put their money behind these growth-based strategies. There was money to be made, and these egomaniacs would recklessly invest in the destruction of the environment.

The problem with degrowth and contraction is that they are not seen as worth investing in, mostly because they actually require little investment. Nobody ever made money from shrinking. The would-be investors of degrowth are absent, and so are the champions, because the main beneficiary of degrowth would not be the investor. It would be the planet. It would be the 8 million species on Earth who would potentially get their planet back. Degrowth can only be investment-worthy if the investors, and all of us, realised that this is not another construction mega-project for the sake of profit. It is a life-and-death initiative to safeguard the future of humanity, as well as the ecosystem that sustains it. What the investors and leaders will never understand is that the benefits of degrowth are neither financial, nor political. They are existential. Little investment is actually needed in order to contract. We are tearing things down, replacing them with lighter structures. This does mean fewer profits, and a simpler lifestyle for all. And this is where, unfortunately, ordinary consumers are likely to agree with the investors: we're not up for it.

Renewable Necrocapitalism

This means that renewable technology is also not a solution, given that it is overwhelmingly seen by investors and politicians alike as an opportunity for growth at the expense of the planet. The implementation of renewable technologies has so far only catered towards meeting an escalating energy demand, while growing a new industrial sector: complete with its own greedy tycoons, its own corrupt lobbyists, and PR misinformation machine. Here we go again. This new industry was needed to replace all those lost fossil fuel jobs, along with the lost lobbying and PR professionals looking for the next big thing to latch on, like desperate leeches searching for blood. The renewable energy industrial complex is providing precisely this opportunity, for millions of these people. The "energy transition" is nothing but the transition of all these fossil fuel-affiliated jobs to a new business opportunity. This is a full-steam growth project as opposed to a degrowth initiative, which follows the familiar recipe of necrocapitalism. We have been scammed yet again by replacement economics. The focus, yet again, is on scaling up energy production rather than addressing the problem of escalating energy demand which brought us to this predicament in the first place.

This explains why the renewables industry does have plenty of stakeholders and champions, who belong in the list of usual suspects and criminals mentioned earlier. Their motivation is personal profit. These stakeholders are in it for the money and for their own benefit, and they do not represent humans, Earth's biome, or a sustainable future. If anything is renewable here, it is necrocapitalism, who has managed to rise up from its own ashes and completely re-invent itself, yet again, through wind farms and electric vehicles that will never be suitably and sustainably recycled. As with previous necrocapitalist developments, the psychonomy needs to placate all consumatrons residing in the farm via a rewards package. For this reason, the Green New Deal vision comes with the promise of jobs and a life of luxury, as these are the only messages the public really wants to hear. Imagine what would happen if one morning suddenly people woke up, realised that the Green New Deal they had been sold was an investor fairy tale with no rewards, and that Earth was in fact doomed unless we scaled down literally everything, starting with our own use of resources. How depressing and unacceptable would that be.

Technologies that can help us get out of this apocalyptic mess do exist, but our problem is who implements them, and how they implement them. There are many truly renewable and sustainable solutions, such as trees, including some which are human-invented. They all immediately become unsustainable and unrenewable however, when implemented with growth, profit and investment in mind by people who have absolutely zero interest in saving this planet. The vacancy for passionate champions for degrowth is still open. Who will fill it?

A Principle Too Altruistic

The conceptual issue with contraction is that it is an overarching principle, not a specific technology. This is a significant departure for a species which has been historically great with technologies, but not so much with ethics and principles. Technologies become viral and thrive, while principles become weaponized and corrupted. However sophisticated and elaborate our civilization becomes, it can never escape the parasite of corruption dwelling in its flesh. This, is the threat to any selfless solution, and degrowth is an incredibly selfless principle whose benefits would reverberate across an entire planet. Are we mature enough to embrace it?

But the choice is clear: we either lose absolutely everything, or we contract and potentially save the planet. It is probably too altruistic a motive for our inward-facing society, as the benefits of degrowth would not filter down to humans exclusively. The benefits would be shared with the rest of the ecosystem, something which humans have never done during their entire existence: to give something back to Earth.

Moreover, the "return of investment", in financial terms, would not be immediate. It would possibly not be felt until generations down the line, given that much of civilisational collapse is already "baked in". However, there would be a non-financial return of investment, which could be almost immediate: less work for all of us, a simpler, happier lifestyle, to start with. And in the long term, a potential planet recovery.

This is why degrowth cannot be discussed in business terms. It is not a venture. It is not a project. It is a principle, a moral one if you like, and a way of being and living our everyday existence which requires waking up from the necrocapitalist matrix. This is why it cannot even be framed within the human economy, as this stands today. It can only be understood within the Earth's economy.

All of this may sadly be too abstract, too "out there" for our mainstream economists to understand, accept, contemplate, and even imagine, when their imagination and ethics were long ago assasinated by an economics academia which preaches to itself the mantras of GDP, profit, growth, necrocapitalism, and the illusion that the human economy is self-contained. Education and academia for that matter, have become a privilege of the elites: the very people who prop-up necrocapitalism. We are increasingly relying on people who have grown up within this system, to write books about changing the system.

The human economy has been in debt ever since its inception. The Earth's economy is the only sustainable economy on the planet, and the BOE (Bank Of Earth) is the only solvent bank that has ever existed on Earth. It is where we have been borrowing from, all of this time, deluding ourselves that we were "growing". We have been in fact growing on borrowed Earth currency, living on credit from the BOE. Humanity aggressively took over the formerly sustainable company of this planet, ascending into CEO with the sole purpose of devouring capital, ripping off stakeholders, and liquidating what was left. The leadership board of this company, now composed entirely of humans, is a criminal organization responsible for the destruction of resources and the willing, deliberate extinction of thousands of species.

Degrowth would, for the first time in millions of years, begin to replenish the BOE's balance sheet of natural resource capacity. But as it stands, the entirety of humanity is against degrowth, for the simple reason that degrowth does not promise immediate, human-specific economic profit. It is difficult to put this message on an election banner. So we'd rather lose it all, than share this planet with the rest of its beings.

Declaration of War Against Profit

It is clear from this conversation that any solution which relies on profit, and on stakeholders who are only interested in profit, is not a solution. It is also evident that there is no immediate money in degrowth, and any gains from it are far too abstract, altruistic and future-focused to ever become attractive as a political campaign or bussiness proposal. Degrowth fails to tick all boxes, when it comes to boosting GDP and fattening the pockets of oligarchs - things which are important to our dystopian social structure, psychonomy, and current system as a whole.

The obstacle to degrowth therefore is profit itself, the very notion of money, and an economic system which keeps humanity hostage to its own incoming Armageddon. We are addicted to profit. At every step of the way, this civilization has consciously opted for meaningless short-term lifestyle benefits, at the expense of existentially disastrous future consequences. These are the exact same priorities as those of a drug addict.

Necrocapitalism is the thief, the oligarch who still operates at large, and who never got caught. As long as the motive is profit, we will continue to fail. No technological know-how, no renewable energy innovation or Green New Deal will ever fix a black heart that wants to exploit, to consume, to turn people and beings into products and profit.

Contraction Isn't Fun. But Neither is Collapse

There is an incredible level of naivety and hypocrisy in the business world regarding sustainability, "Net Zero", and carbon emissions. Most feel it is a case of ticking a few boxes, rather than the massive sacrifice and transformation which contraction requires. Business has developed incredibly sophisticated sustainability campaigns - using money which could have gone towards walking the walk, rather than talking the talk. This is the level of hypocrisy. No business today is actually prepared to go through the sacrifices and the contraction which are part of a degrowth initiative, as this would contradict the very definition of what a business is, and what it does: to grow, indefinitely. Rather than emulating the sustainable ebb and flow of "profit" witnessed in the natural world, global corporate cultures are pretending to be sustainable while still delusionally fixating on the futility of constant growth.

If this civilization had any chance of continuing, it would need to stop laying foundations for a new, bigger empire each time, and start learning the lessons from mourning the one which is already collapsing. True degrowth means reducing all aspects of our presence on Earth. This includes the most important one of all, and the most carbon-heavy, which is our population. The idea of 8 billion planet-eating consumatrons continuing in a world of diminishing resources is yet another ludicrous religious and economic fantasy which has lasted too long for its own good. True environmentalists and economists should talk about the monster of overpopulation. Earth's system did not evolve to cater for a single species of this population size.

Decriminalizing Contraction

Scaling back our impact on this planet goes against everything this civilization was founded upon: scaling up greed, scaling up population, scaling up natural destruction. Degrowth is only possible if we decriminalize contraction, simplification and ecological restoration. For an ecologist, scaling down our consumption, energy use and population growth means finally living in balance with the planet and the climate. For most politicians as well as the public who vote for them, these critical steps will be labelled as a gross infringement on human rights. Those who support these steps simply won't get the votes and will be marginalised as "ecofascists": people who take the side of nature, as if nature is our enemy. Today's politicians after all mirror today's consumatronic humans: they lack all of the qualities that our economic system has successfully exterminated: empathy, critical thinking, and above all, a conscience.

How can degrowth be implemented under these circumstances? It would require everyone having to "wake up" simultaneously. Much of environmental activism seems to focus on the "elites", "corporations" or a handful of "bad guys". But the reality is that the world is enslaved to a system of unsustainable greed in which each of us is an essential participant, whether we benefit from it or not, whether we officially "endorse" it or not. What will likely never be communicated to us by leaders is that true degrowth involves no investors, job creation, green new deals or fancy EVs. It is a sacrifice, which cannot be and should not be sugar-coated to the voters.

But we will never hear this truth. In the 80s the food industry lied to us, replacing fat with sugar rather than advising us to eat less overall. In the 2020s, the renewables industry lied to us, replacing fossil fuels with Tesla cars, rather than telling us to drive less overall.

Mental Inertia

Many naive economists and politicians think they can plan for the disaster that is coming. They think they will continue to have access to budgets, for a "social and economic transition" in the midst of natural disasters, massive global migration, social unrest, hunger and nuclear war. They think they can calculate how much the insurance will cost to rebuild after natural disasters, as if the insurance industry won't have collapsed by then, under the weight of closely-spaced, catastrophic climate events which dwarf in scale what we are used to. Any human currency for that matter, by then, will have lost its value in a world of war, hunger and destruction. What the insurance industry doesn't understand is that, in the face of what is coming, insurance cannot be purchased. Insurance is only earned, by doing the things that prevent natural disasters in the first place. The best insurance is prevention. And it is already getting too late for prevention.

These short-sighted people tucked up in comfy government and think tank positions will be lucky to simply have a job, if governments and contracts still exist. Most of them have already become peons of the renewable energy industrial complex: rather than coming clean about the gravity of the situation, they are trying to sell the beautiful golden sunsets of a Green New Deal, sponsored by the same oligarchs and psychopaths who have been running the world for the last few hundred years. Meanwhile, there are authors and academics so desperate to justify humanity's parasitic existence, all they can come up with is that our purpose on Earth is to become wisdom keepers and stewards of this planet, presiding over this creation. This is the typical ignorant, human supremacist talk of any hallucinating narcissist trying to save face, and refusing to concede failure on behalf of their own species.

Shrink Now, or Collapse Tomorrow

But none of this should be surprising. Throughout our evolution, all we wanted was more comfort, more convenience, more love and affection, and more domination. And whilst we achieved many of these things at incredible scale and speed, we hoarded them all for ourselves, leaving the rest of the planet behind. Obsessed with more efficiency and convenience, we became trapped in a psychosis of greed and acquisition, to the point where we lost sight of who we are, and what we are. At no point in our history did we even consider to share the benefits of our achievements with the rest of the beings of this planet, a great proportion of which we have already made extinct.

It should be deeply worrying that the very species responsible for the decimation of Earth has also arrogantly put itself in charge of rescuing it. If I was the planet, humans would be the last species I would trust to bring me back to health. Degrowth is not a series of boxes to untick. It requires a fundamental change in how we define happiness. It requires the burying and mourning of a lifestyle and colorful vision of our civilization which we all falsely thought was normal, and sustainable. A controlled dismantling of the most wasteful and destructive pieces of our civilization is the bare minimum we ought to do to slow down the climate crisis and ecological overshoot. The alternative is to suffer the most cataclysmic apocalypse which all traditional solutions presented here would result in, and which would surely erase most everything we hold dear.

Mitigating the climate crisis is not a technology fix. There are 8 billion humans living parasitic lifestyles. We would need to bravely accept upfront some level of pain, and voluntarily demolish the ecocidal system this entire civilisation has been based upon - or it crashes down on us. Will the media and politicians treat the public as adults, and tell them the truth? And upon hearing the truth, will the public react as adults? We may never find out. Humans have a bizarre ability in identifying, analysing and recognising all of the things that they are doing wrong, and yet, carry on doing them anyway. It is ironic that a species which prides itself for its science, technology and rational thinking, can't even admit to itself that it has an extremely serious overpopulation problem, leading to its demise. Only if humanity completely demolishes the toxic narratives of supremacy, unlimited growth and progress on which it has built its flimsy house of cards, can it develop new, more egalitarian narratives upon which a completely new, multi-species social and political organization can emerge. One which emulates the actual ecosystem we came from, and which we are still part of. The climate Armageddon we are experiencing is a direct mirror into who we are as a society. As our civilisation overheats from its own by-products, wars and psychoses, so does the planet.

Human civilisation is a firework. It takes a lot of ingenuity, patience, love, technology, cooperation and hard work to set it all up, but only a split second to see it all explode. From the beginning of our journey, we wanted happiness. We wanted love. We wanted "stuff". But we forgot what we had already. And now we risk having nothing left. As our civilisation bubble bursts open, contraction will happen one way or another, whether we consciously pursue it or not.

SELF-HARMING CIVILIZATIONS

Trauma: A Vital Cosmic Experience

Trauma is a part of life. It is what shapes us, what makes us. It teaches us valuable lessons and can transform us into better humans. We all remember a distant childhood memory of falling on the ground, hurting ourselves and crying. We remember how harsh the gravel and dust felt against our fresh, young skin as it tore open and began to bleed. We remember times when we felt embarrassed and wanted to disappear, or times when we were bullied and felt powerless and scared. Etched in my memory will be the time when I was stood up on a date and felt angry and worthless, or that afternoon when I got fired from work, right before Christmas. Twice.

Although we will never be the same after a traumatic experience, trauma always presents us with an opportunity to become a new, stronger and wiser version of ourselves. Trauma is perhaps the most effective way in which humans and other animals learn. It has powerful, transformative and regenerative effects on the psyche and spirit, which go beyond a simple learning experience. It is common knowledge that people who have lost something or someone are wiser and nicer overall. They tend to be less arrogant, more empathetic, more open, maybe because they don't want others to ever feel the way that they felt, when they suffered trauma or loss.

But most of all, they seem to radiate some type of quiet, infinite wisdom which connects them to everything around them. When you look into their eyes, you can sometimes see pieces of the universe. This is because their trauma has opened a door to a consciousness which transcends time and space. Our entire universe, including Earth, is made out of trauma and chaos. If we feel no connection to this trauma, we are unable to understand our world. Trauma may be a door which all of us cross in different ways, but all of us have the potential to emerge on the other side more enlightened, connected and whole than ever before, even as we break into a million pieces.

Trauma's transformative power only becomes available to us when we are brave enough to let it take over us, allowing it to pass through our body like electricity. If we try and suppress, deny or compartmentalise it however, trauma becomes trapped inside our body. It begins to boil under our skin, where it becomes responsible for strange psychosomatic reactions, often autoimmune, and behaviours which end up potentially inflicting the same exact trauma on others. Unprocessed trauma inflicts most of its damage months, even years after the initial traumatic event. Sometimes it is even inherited from parents to children, burdening unsuspecting victims with unresolved family trauma going back to events which took place multiple generations ago. Sometimes it affects entire communities, or even ecosystems. Earth itself in its an entirety is a superorganism, exhibiting the same psychosomatic responses all organisms exhibit. What climate scientists often describe as unexplainable, off-the-chart climate data, is nothing but the result of the planet's accumulated trauma finally finding a way to manifest itself.

The negative emotions associated with trauma are only the door which leads to the rest of the journey. This is why these painful emotions need to be felt, as much as this is a terrifying experience. If we bravely surrender to trauma, powerful psychological mechanisms are activated which resemble a near-death experience, giving new insights into ourselves and into our place in the world. They give us access to a new consciousness, which connects us to every single trauma that has existed in the billions of years this planet has existed. Trauma has the power to connect us, because it is something we all share. Through each traumatic experience we become time travelers, connected to the world, to every single plant, animal, insect or bacterium who has ever gone through a life-threatening experience.

By allowing ourselves to feel all of this, we begin to slowly see the other side of the tunnel, as we connect to an ancient cycle of death and regeneration which we have in common with all forms of biological existence. Our traumatic experience becomes so much more than just learning "what to avoid next time". It becomes a spiritual transformation to a new existence which resides outside of our ego. We become more open, aware, introspective, connected and compassionate. We become time and space. We become whole, and more resilient.

Breaking The Cycle

Most religions have created narratives and imagery which tried to tap into the incredible potential of unresolved, raw trauma, with the aim of manipulating us towards their version of salvation: from the crucifixion and resurrection of Jesus, to

Karma and reincarnation. But trauma is and should be a personal experience, not an organised religion. Trauma can only achieve its transformative potential if the one traumatized allows their unpleasant experience to humble them, rather than intimidate them into submission. It is about exposing ourselves to our own fragility, our imperfection, and our insignificance within the larger universe.

Most of all, it is about accepting that trauma is a part of life. It is not about resisting it, but learning to live with it. Although it may feel like a deeply personal experience, it is important to remember that trauma did not only happen to us. It happens to millions of people, every day. In this sense, we are not alone. We are part of a cycle, part of a common pool of trauma which may affect us disproportionately at certain times. But we are not isolated.

Once we realise how universal trauma is we can begin to close the tortuous cycle of trauma and violence. There are no bullies and victims. Everyone at some point becomes a victim and has the potential to also be a bully. By connecting with our inner world, as well as recognising the trauma that naturally surrounds us everywhere, we begin to see how bullies and victims are actually two sides of the same coin. Then, and only then, do we begin to make a conscious choice: are we a bully, a victim, or simply an enlightened being? Trauma, when fully processed, allows us to rise above this cycle between bully and victim so that it does not affect us as much. It eventually becomes a triumph over the futile, exhausting competition we have with our own ego, as we try to mask our trauma through external pursuits.

This awareness can become a celebration of our mortality, of the present, and of our life force which is so much more intimately connected with the rest of the planet's beings, than we would ever have imagined. This new consciousness in turn can arm us with the defiance and determination to remain connected to the present, and become resilient to incoming trauma, no matter the circumstances. More importantly, it allows us to end the tortuous cycle of self-harm, which unprocessed trauma often brings.

Unprocessed Trauma Is A Prison

Failing to recognize that we have been traumatized in the first place robs us of all this vital insight, preventing us from moving forward. The wounds may appear to have healed, but deep down we are still tormented, guided by fear as our compass. Unable to fully come to grips with, and manage our trauma, we end up settling for a substandard life within an equally traumatized (and traumatic) world, where the psychonomy is able to monetize our unhealthy psychology. We surrender to this environment, limping through life while pursuing material and professional success in order to try and forget the damaged parts of ourselves.

Before we know it, we have entered the vicious bully-victim cycle again, inflicting back onto the world the unprocessed trauma we sustained ourselves. Preoccupied by this toxic cycle, rather than choosing to walk away from it altogether, we become blind to the vastness of time and space that is available to us. We become limited, failing to see other options, and end up accepting life as a series of terrifying, nail-biting and self-limiting moments of anguish. Sometimes we move to the very opposite end, resorting to hedonism and denial as our only ways of coping with the trauma which is a natural part of life.

We don't have to choose either of these two extreme scripts, which are part of the same coin of denial anyway. The truth lies somewhere in the uncomfortable, uneasy and vague space between the two: between anguish and joy. Our challenge, the challenge of any organism, is to maintain its balance between these two extremes. Happiness is not the pursuit of joy. It is the successful integration of both joyful and traumatic experiences into our life, and the reconciliation with the fact that both of these will always be present in some form.

Self-Harm As A Distraction

Unable to process its trauma, our civilization has been applying technological bandages in the hope of making an otherwise chaotic life more convenient. But convenience is a trap, as much as it brings tangible benefits to our everyday practical existence. Genuine existential fulfillment has been sacrificed in the altar of a never-ending pointless quest for luxury. But this was only an engineered distraction to help us avoid dealing with our trauma and existential fears. We became restless consumers going around in circles, conveniently blind both towards our inner selves as well as the natural world we had all come from. Sinking ourselves further into denial and distraction as the industrial revolution brought trauma upon trauma on us which we simply could not process, we stopped paying attention to our inner world, our feelings, our fears, our intuitions, allowing the psychonomy to tell us what to feel instead. But a civilisation which casually walks into the darkness without its heart is a walking corpse. In the name of efficiency, convenience and productivity, humans have long ago stopped asking themselves: what makes me truly happy?

Luxury and convenience have nothing to do with happiness, and they certainly do not help us process or break the cycle of trauma that still lingers. The more convenience we achieved, ironically the more task-oriented and transactional our lives became, oversaturating us while at the same time shutting us down, to the point of cognitive unconsciousness. An unconscious being cannot access its trauma. A psychotherapy industry worth billions has been set up just so that people can find the time to ask themselves a few simple existential questions that all of us should have been asking daily. This industry is merely scratching the surface, as trauma layered upon trauma conceals our basic fear: mortality.

Rather than addressing their trauma and mortality, human civilizations have always sought to distract themselves from their existential issues by shifting their attention to building crystal castles. Our greed, arrogance, and their negative effects on the planet are symptoms of an ego that is unable to face its fear of death. The more the ego is unable to deal with its fears, the more it seeks dangerous and unhealthy distractions. We have been on a frenetic quest to prove to ourselves that we are invincible and infallible, and in fact, immortal. Yet in the course of this quest, we have created a civilization that traumatizes us, every single day.

This is the tragic paradox of all the "amenities" we have built for ourselves. The more we cover up our trauma, the more unconscious we become. The more unconscious we become, ironically, the more new trauma we can tolerate. We keep on creating more trauma, then smothering it up in sugar and entertainment so that we can add more trauma on top. These are the pain-numbing, coping strategies of our time. It is a perverse addiction which has rendered us truly unconscious to the trauma we are inflicting both upon ourselves and upon this planet.

Death-Worshipping Civilisations

Our dysfunctional relationship with trauma has also shaped our very perception of what constitutes progress. Rather than focusing on technologies and innovations which increase our overall mental and physical well-being, our civilizations have been focusing for much too long on building exploitative and self-destructive economic systems which increase, rather than reduce trauma. The quest for efficiency, convenience and profit has overtaken the primary goal of all humans to live a happy, balanced, and meaningful existence. Instead of embarking on a journey towards existential inner balance, we have a civilization which keeps inventing new ways to conceal its trauma, rather than consciously process it. Our consumption-driven society offers us an unlimited range of unhealthy psychological coping mechanisms which aim to deal with, and distract us from, our unprocessed fear of death and the ephemeral nature of our existence. This comes with a spiraling denial of death itself, which only further increases our insecurity, restlessness and desperation to find ever more new ways and technologies to convince ourselves that we are happy, and immortal. All of these coping mechanisms are short-lived of course, and unable to plug a widening existential void which we have never really addressed, ever since the beginning of our evolution into organised societies.

Our inability to accept death has ironically resulted in a civilisation which worships it. Whether it means building more empires, destroying more natural resources, shopping, or using drugs, this civilization is desperately trying to distract itself from the fear of its own long-term unsustainability. Greed, unscrupulous growth, and the pursuit of success at all costs, have been the psychological coping mechanisms helping us avoid, at all costs, staying in the moment for just one second, and simply being with ourselves: be with our mortality, and begin to truly value not only our own life, but all forms of life which exist on the planet.

The tragic irony is that all of these unhealthy coping mechanisms are self-harming, as well as destructive to Earth. It is a tragedy that the more we refuse to process our fear of death and trauma, the more we create civilizations which worship death and destruction. We are recycling our unprocessed trauma in order to keep ourselves distracted from facing our original fears, like an adult trying to relive a painful childhood experience. We have trapped ourselves in a vicious cycle: from traumatized, we have become the traumatizers. Part of us is trying to recreate our trauma, because deep down we know that only through processing it can we ever feel truly alive, truly ourselves. Instead, we have become a blind killing machine, destroying everything that moves, lives and breathes. This is the recurring cycle of trauma which we have trapped ourselves in.

Estranged From Ourselves

As an increasingly panicking humanity runs away from the fires it has set, the risk is that it will continue to look outside for solutions, rather than within itself. It will continue to set off more fires and engage in even more irrational behavior, finding refuge from its unprocessed trauma in the coping mechanisms, technologies and dictators who will validate and exploit its fears, all the while as the cycle of trauma continues. This is unfortunately what all trauma does: it isolates us from both our true self, and the people who could potentially help us.

Humanity today is not simply in denial of its predicament. It has stopped paying attention altogether, self-medicating with celebrity news just as it circles the drain of it's own information black hole. This civilisation will go down very fast if we continue on this path. How much more pain do we need to feel, or to inflict on ourselves and the world around us, so that we can wake up to the toxic cycle we have trapped ourselves in?

Our restlessness and insecurity have resulted in a civilization maddened with toxic ambition. In this "always on", 24-hour society we have created, we have forbidden ourselves to ever sit still, in the fear that we might become aware of our mortality and fragility - or god forbid, begin to question our manufactured, consumer "theme park" reality. We despise sitting still as a form of laziness, and our obsession with ambition and destruction has brought about a sleeplessness epidemic, causing anxiety and depression to skyrocket. We take mindfulness meditation courses just so that we can remember what it used to feel like to simply sit still, to need nothing else but our own breath, our own existence in order to feel complete. We are beginning to deny ourselves our basic biological functions, including the capacity for emotion. But if we lose the ability to feel, we will never be able to process our trauma.

Ashamed Of Our Roots

In our quest for immortality, we have almost sought to convince ourselves that we are not from Earth, therefore not mortal. The industrial revolution, the look and feel of our modern cities, our cars, our houses, have all served to try and convince us that we are not even related to everything else that lives and breathes on this planet. We are made of glass and steel, not flesh, bones, feelings, fears, and sensitivities. We refuse to be reminded that we are as fragile as the 8 million species we have subjugated on this planet. Our denial of our mortality has meant that we have constructed civilizations which nurture contempt for nature, and the natural cycle of death and rebirth which is part of Earth. Our civilizations look to shield us, and distract us from anything which will remind us that we are in fact, from Earth: that at some point way back, we came from the "wild", out of the jungles and savannahs, just like all the other beings - and that this is where all of our molecules will return when we die.

The image of nature as an "unruly wilderness" is of course a fraudulent human narrative. Nature is a product of careful, conscious, natural evolution over billions of years, which followed a precise set of physical laws respecting the stability, sustainability and circularity of energy, water, and life itself. Nature is not an accident. Nature is a product of the laws of physics, and it is precisely because of these laws that it has an incredible ability to find its balance and recover, if only it was left alone. Nature's economy doesn't need electricity, jobs, money or supermarket food. It doesn't fret constantly about its GDP. It already has its own grassroots-powered political system, and the perfect resource-based economy. Through the Earthnet of Things, this planet is 100% connected, conscious, and aware of any imbalances around the clock, which it actions immediately. The natural ecosystem which we consider "wild", is in fact the only truly intelligent, sustainable and self-aware civilization that has ever existed on this planet.

We tend to shun nature and the natural ecosystem precisely because they remind us of who we are and where we came from. Yet in our quest to shield ourselves from mortality, we created polluted cities which are toxic to all biological life, including our own. Our psychonomy traumatizes us with meaningless soul-sucking "bullshit jobs" which only push paper and CO_2 around the globe, and end up pushing us towards burnout, for the reward of a salary that enslaves us to the consumatron farm.

As this self-harming civilization becomes increasingly toxic to us, to the planet, and to all life, it will need to keep devising more narratives, more coping mechanisms, more consumer rewards programs and entertainment technologies to keep us within its grip of trauma denial: until the day when it unavoidably comes face to face with its own, sudden, death. Our only defense is to begin questioning every single aspect of the pre-rehearsed, pre-packaged and mass manufactured life that the psychonomic farm has put together for us to follow, down to the last detail. Because obviously, this life has failed.

UNDER THE WATCHFUL GAZE OF
THE EARTHNET OF THINGS

Necrocapitalism may have reached sentience, but there is another sentient system on this planet that is much, much older. In fact, it is ancient. It is billions of years old. The rocks that fall off a cliff, the sea kelp that grows in the ocean, the light of the sun sweeping over land in the morning as it sneaks in between passing clouds, are all part of this sentient system. They all talk to each other in ways that are more clear, more honest, more direct and more unambiguous than any human language. They are all part of one, massive, complex supercomputer which connects the weather system, ecosystem, and all geological and physical processes that take place on this planet. They are part of the Earthnet of Things.

I have previously referenced the EoT both in my book The Unhappiness Machine and the novella A New Earth, but have never fully explained to my readers what it is, partly because I struggled to put it into words. It would be like explaining the Universe: one can only be in awe of such a vast, beautiful being.

The Earthnet of Things is not just the planet's operating system. It is not a machine or algorithm. It is an actual brain that thinks, and even feels. It responds to stimuli and disturbances, as messages constantly flow between its trillions of components. It is an orchestra that is able to adjust the beat of its song or correct it, and bring it back into line if one of the leading instruments goes off-note. It can retune itself if it has to, in any which way out of billions of possible configurations. The EoT is truly intelligent, and self-aware.

Sometimes it may take many years to close a communication loop, but messages within the EoT are never lost. Nothing goes unnoticed, simply because everything within the EoT is under surveillance, while at the same time having the important role of surveilling everything else. Such is the level of interconnectedness. The EoT represents all the chemical elements, physical components, energies and capabilities within

Earth. It can sense both big and small disturbances. It knows when one of its 8 million species has gone missing. Earth itself is a superorganism, exhibiting the same psychosomatic responses all organisms exhibit. What climate scientists describe as unexplainable, off-the-chart climate data, is nothing but the result of the planet's accumulated trauma finally manifesting itself.

As a matter of fact the EoT represents the whole of Earth and everything that is in it and on it: there isn't one single object, organism or other entity, not even a light evening air breeze that isn't part of the Earthnet of Things. The EoT is everything, and everything is the EoT. Everyone in it has a part to play, however big or small.

Most importantly, the various components of the EoT do not simply talk to each other. They report into each other, whether they like to or not. Even Humanity, and Necrocapitalism are components of the EoT, albeit unwilling ones. Their deeds have severe impacts on the planet which have already warranted a response, as the orchestra searches for a new song which will fit its current mood. Humanity, and the Thing it has created, have hijacked this symphony. But they won't be orchestra conductors for very long. As more and more instruments go extinct, the cacophony of sound will kill the conductor. A new song will rise out of the ashes one day, as the EoT reconstitutes itself.

Earth now needs to protect the malnourished children she has left, from the one child hoarding resources and killing all the others. The EoT is mobilizing, the furniture of the planet's weather is being rearranged. Humans already have no place in this overheating house. 200 thousand years of modern human occupation on Earth are coming to a pivotal moment. We either recognise the sovereignty of the biocivilization we destroyed and begin making reparations, or witness the spectacular fall of the brutal regime which has oppressed all life forms.

Humans have been depleting the BOE for thousands of years, without making any deposits. Withdrawal limit has been breached. The bank account is closing. And 8 million other species are waiting for their money back. Our one and only lender, Earth, has already begun confiscating assets in order to minimize exposure to human debt. The bailiffs are at our doorstep with an eviction notice and an empty truck waiting outside. The human lending experiment is over. Time to recoup losses, and close this account.

Thank you for reading. If you think this book is worth discovering by others, please spread the word or take a few moments to rate it or write a review.

BOOKS BY THIS AUTHOR

The Unhappiness Machine

A New Earth

Pocket Philosophy For End Times

Poems For A Planet Running Out Of Time

Photographic Heart: Tales Of The Earth And The Sea

Printed in Great Britain
by Amazon